the other mother

THE OTHER MOTHER

How to Be an Almost Perfect Mother-In-Law

YVETTE STRAUSS

Impact Publishers®
SAN LUIS OBISPO, CALIFORNIA 93406

Impact Publishers and colophon are registered trademarks of Impact Publishers, Inc.

Library of Congress Cataloging-in-Publication Data

Strauss, Yvette.
    The other mother : how to be an almost perfect mother-in-law /
Yvette Strauss.
      p.   cm.
    Includes bibliographical references and index.
    ISBN 0-915166-98-4 (pbk. : alk. paper)
    1. Mother-in-law.   I. Title.
HQ759.25.S77   1996
646.7'8—dc20   96-10874
                                              CIP

Printed in the United States of America on acid-free paper
Cover design by Sharon Schnare, San Luis Obispo, California
Published by **Impact** ◈ **Publishers** ®
        POST OFFICE BOX 1094
    SAN LUIS OBISPO, CALIFORNIA 93406

Contents

Foreword

Introduction

1. WITCHES, DRAGONS, AND OTHER MYTHS   *1*

2. QUILTS, SCRIPTS, AND SCAPEGOATS
   Becoming "The Other Mother"   *15*

3. WHOSE DREAMS?
   The Other Mother Chronicles   *33*

4. "THY PEOPLE SHALL BE MY PEOPLE"
   Marriage and Mothers-In-Law Across Cultures   *57*

5. NOT-QUITE IN-LAWS:
   When your Child Is Not Married   *91*

6. BRIDGING THE COMMUNICATION GAP:
   *The Other Mother's Guide to When and
   How to Speak Up... or Shut Up*   *115*

7. FROM EXPECTATION TO REALITY
   "This Is Not What I Thought It Would Be Like"   *141*

8. FROM THE BOTTOM OF YOUR HEART
   Gift-Giving for the Other Mother   *157*

9. IMPROVING YOUR IN-LAW IMAGE:
   *It's Time to Become the Person
   You've Always Wanted to Be*   *175*

10. FRIENDSHIP —
    Thoughts on the Care & Feeding of Relationships   187

11. GROWING
    It Takes a Lot of Loving to Become Real   197

Epilogue   213
    The "Seven Deadly Sins" of Mothers-in-Law

    Twelve Traits of Almost-Perfect Mothers-in- Law

Bibliography   215

Index   219

Foreword

*T*he Other Mother is a book written for the millions of mothers-in-law who fend for themselves but don't have much guidance in doing it successfully. With compassion Yvette Strauss helps her readers to enrich the second half of life by teaching them how to build and maintain the best possible relationships with their married children. The reader learns how she can more accurately assess the interactions in a family, in order to improve them. Ms. Strauss encourages us to scrutinize and understand our own behaviors, wisely knowing that only then can positive change occur.

Mothers-in-law are shown how to take control of their lives, even though they are in the midst of significant loss... loss of youth, looks, hormones, and children... and to gain mastery over those losses, discovering the most powerful changes are those that you make within yourself.

This is not a guide to be read and put aside. Initially, it can be digested alone and mulled over; then you can use it for discussion, pondering the suggestions in the company of other mothers-in-law. This book calls for dialogue, because it explores a universal stage of development that has not, until now, been taken very seriously. Mothers-in-law are continually depicted in our society as annoying, intrusive, and often pathetic. Contrary to this notion, we women, in the second half of life, have an enormous potential for being good role models and for sharing our wisdom. Ms. Strauss points out the possible pitfalls with in-law children relationships. She then creates new pathways for our feeling more appreciated, contented, and empowered.

For those mothers-in-law whose children have chosen partners outside their own ethnic group or partners of the same sex, this book also provides an opportunity to look at some differences among people... allowing a new way of life to become less foreign, less fearful, and therefore, more understandable and acceptable.

Although Yvette Strauss is not a professional psychotherapist, she is a mother-in-law and has had a mother-in-law. Her writing comes from the heart, and is informed by a foundation of many years training as a volunteer in the mental health field. By helping mothers-in-law have a better relationship with their in-law children, Ms. Strauss shows us a way to improve lives. Her easy to use techniques are practical and understandable; they reach to the core of our existence.

— *Felice Toonkel, M.Ed., CCMHC, PsyA.*

Acknowledgements

This book was not a solo effort. Many individuals have made essential contributions, and I want to thank them.

First, I am enormously grateful for the brilliance and unfailing support of my friend Felice Toonkel, psychoanalyst and clinical mental health counselor, who, from the very inception of this project, has been my mentor. With sensitivity and wisdom, she has labored through each chapter with me, and her thoughts not only enriched the book but opened my mind and heart.

A special thank-you goes to Dr. Max Goldberg, psychiatrist, on the faculty of Columbia Presbyterian Hospital Psychoanalytic Center, New York, for reading every word and for his wise recommendations. He, too, helped me reach for the stars.

I also want to thank Dr. Jerome Blass, practicing psychologist and psychotherapist, who, with a marvelous sense of humor, researched concepts, responded to questions, and offered suggestions; Michelle Seligman, a talented marital and family therapist, who shared with me helpful ideas whenever needed; and Dr. Jean McNally, internist, who advised me on psychosomatic illness and offered suggestions.

My gratitude goes as well to Rabbi Naftali Brawer for sharing his expertise about Lubavitcher Jews with me.

Rachel Knobler, who was my coordinator at the Bergen County Parent Workshop, sat with me for hours being creative; I want to thank her for her assistance, perceptive insights, invaluable clarity, warmth, and for the special friendship that evolved during the writing of this book.

Grace Gartner and Harriet Held gave this project constructive criticism and ideas. Their thoughts enriched this manuscript and helped me put into precise words paragraphs that were obscure. Thank you for your unending support.

I'd also like to thank Barry Sheinkopf, who helped me edit this manuscript, for his expert advice and encouragement; and Bob Alberti, my publisher, whose editorial input added great verve to the text.

Thank-you to Carole Abel, Anita Becker, Bea Berson, Miranda Black, Miriam Cusmariu, Carol Dervitz, Pat Dickinson, Marlene Goldberg, Arlene Handler, Soon Juhng, Scott Kennedy, Florence Leeds, Denise Niclas, Ruth Paci, Charles Passaggio, Virginia Passaggio, Rita Posner, Steve Redish, Carol Reiman, Joyce Rosen, Nancy Ryan, and Madeline Vilmos for their invaluable assistance.

I also want to express my deep appreciation to all those whom I interviewed, too numerous to mention here, who shared their thoughts and parts of their lives with me. Their names, and some of the content of their interviews, have been altered to preserve the anonymity of my subject; in any case, their stories are only intended to illustrate general principles of behavior.

All errors or omissions in the text, however, are mine — and are slips of the mind, not of the heart.

I am enormously grateful to my children, who not only helped me grow but listened to me talk about this book for years. To my daughter, who has been enthusiastic about my project from the start and who, each time we spoke, said, "Ma, you can do it," and to my son and daughter-in-law, heartfelt thanks.

Finally, to my husband, I offer a special thank-you, not only for his invaluable ideas and patience, but for his help in critiquing, his warm heart and his incredible faith. Without it, this book would never have become a reality.

— *Yvette Strauss*

*Dedicated to the memory of
my mother-in-law, Rebecca Strauss*

Introduction

*I*s any group the target of more jokes than mothers-in-law? When is the last time you said — or thought — something positive about your own mother-in-law? And, when it comes to identifying people you admire and care for, how high is your mother-in-law on the list?

Have you thought about why? What is it about mothers-in-law that gives them such a bad reputation in our society?

Think about it. You're forty-five or so. You've raised two children, seen them succeed more-or-less at school, college and beginning career. Now suddenly the oldest (or not) comes home and says, "Guess what, Ma? I'm getting married!" Next thing you know, a daughter- or son-in-law has been added to your family. You didn't ask for it. You didn't even get to choose the person. But you're going to have to live with this new relationship for a long time — probably for the rest of your life.

Those of us who have lived to see children grown and married want to maintain ties with them. Technologically, it's easier than ever now days — out of sight no longer means out of mind. *Successful* communication with your married children is another matter. Once you are in touch, whether face-to-face or voice-to-voice, the possibilities for disagreement and conflict are great.

The complicated job of being a mother-in-law stretches the spirits. At its best, the job can warm our souls; even at worst, it need not scar them with ill-will.

The Other Mother

It's easy to find information on how to be a *mother* today. There is, after all, a new respect for mothers — their worth has grown, especially in the eyes of those fathers who are sharing the responsibility for child rearing. But for anxious, struggling *mothers-in-law,* it's another story. Hardly anybody cares.

Never mind that all mothers-in-law are mothers, and that "mother knows best." Mothers-in-law, who execute the most demanding and unsung of human roles, are hacked away at, caricatured, considered victims to demean. Although the charges in most cases are unfair, a mother-in-law is rarely given a chance to respond, and she has to work twice as hard for any kind of positive recognition.

My own mother-in-law, surrounded by an out-spokenly candid husband and three loving sons, struggled too, when she ventured forth into this territory. I'm sure of that now but in those early days I had no comprehension of what was happening. As a young woman, shy with strangers but filled with an intense desire to please, all I knew was that I yearned to be accepted by that resilient, unspoiled female in her sixties with years of experience behind her.

Although I would never admit it, I was in awe of her. She frightened me when I met my husband's family; she made me feel as if my legs were encased in concrete. But the house revolved around her. Like many new daughters-in-law, I was intimidated by the power she commanded and uneasy in her presence. That wasn't her fault, of course.

I was unformed, vulnerable, not yet truly separated from my own mother (although, like most young brides, I *thought* I was).

Uninitiated in the ways of modern psychology, my mother-in-law was not a woman given to understanding, nor did she hand out compliments when others (*I*) needed them. A Lithuanian immigrant who had known starvation and fear in her youth — suffering I can't fathom — she valued her children above all else. She was a blur of movement, always in the kitchen, cooking for a large family who came and went haphazardly. Food was her way of caring, of saying "I love you" to all she knew.

Her sons would yell, "Ma, where's the salt?" and she'd zoom into the dining room with the shaker while they ate and laughed. Unbidden but taken for granted, she'd stride through the door with tureens of soup and platters of vegetables, meat, and fish, herself not eating until the meal was finished, and then savoring only left-overs.

Even now I find it uncomfortable to refer to Rebecca by her first name; then, it was unthinkable. My mother-in-law was "Mama" to me. I think that name pleased her, although we never talked about it. Generational differences intruded. How little we understood each other. What did I know of her feelings? I didn't understand my own. Feelings were not something one explored in my family, especially with a mother-in-law. But in spite of that, I sensed a genuine warmth between us.

Whenever I think of her today, the image includes her food parcels, lovingly known in the family as "Becky Bags," big brown bundles containing a myriad of items that she dragged with her wherever she went. We, her in-law children, laughed at them, but always looked forward to finding out what treasures they contained when she visited.

I see her shoulders moving from left to right, legs marbled with varicose veins tightly encased in Ace bandages, entering my apartment in days I can never go back to. More often than not, she was pulling a metal wagon overflowing with coffee, brown-spotted bananas, hard candy, chicken, individually wrapped lamb chops "for the baby," soap, Jell-O in all six flavors it came in then, and special cookies that, although they were actually from the bakery, are even today known in our family as "Grandma Becky's cookies."

What she really brought was her love. We never thought about that, but we accepted it and looked forward to it, all the while laughing at Rebecca and her bags. But her legacy goes on, for I am packing Becky bags today. They have traveled through the generations.

In those days, I didn't think of myself as lucky to have this kind of mother-in-law. In fact, I never thought about mothers-in-law at all then. I'm sorry it took so long, but I do appreciate and respect her now — now that I've been transported to that place that Rebecca departed from years ago. Perhaps the adage is true that you have to walk in other people's shoes to understand their problems. I am walking in my mother-in-law's shoes today, and I realize now that they're not comfortable. You don't "just do it." It's tough to be a mother-in-law.

So I dedicate this book to Rebecca, because our culture cries out today for family unity, something she knew much about. Both of us sensed then that our connection wasn't perfect — although it constantly grew with the years. This book, too, is about connecting and growing, about being human, and taking the steps needed to improve relationships between the generations.

About This Book

The Other Mother is an examination of the "bad guy" role into which mothers-in-law have been cast, and a guide to the perplexed. It's a book about losses and gains, and who you are, and who your children are, and how to anticipate — and prevent — problems before they occur.

It's about strangers getting to know one other, human beings who bring to their relationships a full complement of old baggage: for you, forty or more years of emotional needs and deep-rooted convictions to sort out; for your son or daughter-in-law, twenty or thirty years of hidden agendas and strong personal ties that hang in the background; and each of you unaware that you may still be acting out in the present unresolved conflicts of times past.

I don't claim *The Other Mother* to be a one-shot cure or a miracle drug, nor that by reading it *anyone* can be an "almost perfect" mother-in-law. You have to do the work to be successful, and there *is* work to be done.

What you can expect from this book — which I wrote with input from therapists, doctors and dozens of in-law parents and children — is advice to help mothers-in-law lower walls, cope with problems and self-doubts.

We'll explore together the myths, misconceptions, cartoon characters, and hurtful jokes that have formed society's definition of "mother-in-law."

I hope to provide some insights to help you identify your strengths and weaknesses. You'll find communication techniques and explanations to help you change unproductive ways of thinking and find solutions to conflict. One chapter explores the role of mothers-in-law in different cultures — what to expect and what is expected.

With its focus on love, it will offer practical ways to get through a sea of stressful situations so you won't lose your children and grandchildren. I hope you'll come away with determination to find and trust your real self, to allow yourself to grow into a wise woman. After all, life itself is a learning experience. With sensitivity and well-honed mother-in-law skills, you can learn to circumvent misunderstandings, and become successful at making the relationship with your in-law child a satisfying one.

I wish you well on the journey we're about to take together.

Chapter 1

...In which we encounter WITCHES, DRAGONS, AND OTHER MYTHS

...by the time you are Real, most of your hair has been loved off, and your eyes drop out and you get loose in the joints and very shabby. But these things don't matter at all, because once you are Real you can't be ugly, except to people who don't understand...
— Margery Williams, *The Velveteen Rabbit*

I belong to a club — a non-exclusive club made up of millions of *bad women*.

We didn't set out to be bad. We don't enjoy that description. In fact, in most cases it's not even accurate. But we're America's *mothers-in-law* and, in this country at least, that term brings with it an alias: "the bad guys." No matter what we do, the term, *mother-in-law* seems always to carry a negative connotation. Sadly, the label can panic the most accomplished of women.

And why not? The role is thankless enough, and there are lots of obstacles to overcome if you want to be a *good* mother-in-law. Learning how to deal with the person your child has married, and that person's family, will be hard work. Most people — even lots of mothers-in-law — have a deeply entrenched attitude about the job. And then there are the jokes; endless bad jokes at the expense of every "other mother."

But if you do the job well, the rewards of being a successful mother-in-law can be enormous. You'll collide with all kinds of problems, cobble together all sorts of compromises, and launch a long process of asking questions. You'll be growing toward wisdom.

If you can learn to let go, if you will work to form new bonds, if you *believe* you can be a successful — even an almost-perfect — mother-in-law, this book can help you make it happen.

It's Not Just "Because You're a Woman" Any More

A new respect for mothers has flowered in America in recent years. The job of "mother" is no longer devalued; the social worth of the role seems to have expanded. Somehow, however, this beneficence hasn't extended to *mothers-in-law*. Peculiar, isn't it, considering how sensitive we've all become to women's perspectives and rights?

The mother-in-law's role is not easy at best, of course, and it arrives, for most women, at a particularly difficult time. She is coping with the onset of menopause — hot flashes and blue feelings — when every day the mirror brings her face to face with aging.

Actually, mothers-in-law have to deal with *two* major life changes simultaneously, both involving loss, and both painful: *saying good-bye to a child* and *saying good-bye to fertility*. The process leaves most of us emotionally vulnerable and maligned. With no experience in either role, and mired in confusion, we have somehow to fend for ourselves. Also, because we are beginning to show some signs of maturity (let's face it, we're *aging*), society tends to assume that we no longer have much to offer.

No surprise then, that self-esteem suffers: society devalues us, and we in turn value ourselves less.

Very little helpful information exists — no courses, few books, an occasional magazine article. Nonetheless, despite all that's happening to us, we learn and we cope — some by feeling our way in the dark, most driven by past patterns.

Welcome to the Land of Fairy Tales

"Past patterns," unfortunately, do not always serve us well. Still, it's not easy to let go of the familiar messages we collected growing up, those family and societal aphorisms, truths, and myths that taught us how to behave, and warned us to avoid danger at all costs. They were comfortable, self-destructive though they may have been, and today many of us still find it difficult to get beyond them; to see how silly the "perfect family" television programs were; to recognize the problems in our own families; to see through society's simplistic mores and values. After all, as children, they looked real enough and right enough to us, and we bought into them. Women always marry, settle down, and live happily ever after. Don't they?

Hey, we even believed in magic.

We worried about poor Cinderella — would she be able to handle her ambitious step-mother, make it home in time from the ball, before the clock struck twelve, or would she be found out by her cruel family? Of course, Cinderella always managed to prevail. And when she did — and was rescued by the prince — didn't we beam at her triumph, delighted that she lived happily ever after? "Read it again, Mommy!"

Today, most of us no longer buy into fairytales, and we now realize that real people don't usually live "happily ever after," but we still long for the old dreams to be true. We hold on to our cherished myths. They're a part of our history, the messages recorded in our brain — memorized because we heard them so many times — and they are difficult to give up.

Marriage, we learned back in the fifties and sixties, was the answer to solving problems — the path to self-fulfillment. Even today, it is not uncommon for young people to buy into this claim. For my generation, however, marriage was the *perfect escape myth* — so we went searching for a handsome prince who would rescue us from a life of discord, perhaps an unhappy home, maybe abusive parents. Ideally, his strengths would balance our weaknesses and make everything wonderful, and we would be "good" and act "nice" and enjoy life "happily ever after."

That was what most of us wanted to believe.

Witches, Dragons...

As we tried to find our places in the sun, what happened to the real-life angers, frustrations, disappointments, the grief we had to deal with before we got married? They got buried in our psyches — the deepest part of ourselves, only to surface much later.

Life confronts us regularly with relationship problems. We must either work through them or find other ways to contend with them. "Working through" is not easy — insight takes time and risk, lowers our defenses, and raises our anxiety. So we invent a mythology to explain away the problems. As in fairy tales, these myths help us avoid exposing truths about ourselves. We want complex things as simple as possible, so we continue to accept what we learned as little children: to see things as black or white, good or evil, right or wrong.

As adults, most of us learn that only death is absolute, and that many of the messages we received and believed as children were inappropriate and outmoded props on this brief stage.

Yet many of us still act today as we did when we were children, some out of a sense of low self-esteem, others because they prefer not to face facts. We sometimes forget that there are good and bad, destructive and life-affirming aspects in everyone.

In our search for simple solutions, we toss away whole human beings, assigning mythic roles to the characters in our own dramas: the "perfect" mother, the "imperfect" mother-in-law, the "perfect" daughter, the "imperfect" daughter-in-law.

It's not that simple, of course. People are not stick figures, but complex human beings. Fairy tale characters merely fulfill our own wishes. They don't acknowledge the real person. No one is all good or all bad; each human being is made up of a rainbow of colors.

Here are a few of the common mythical qualities of mothers-in-law. I'm sure you've heard most of them:

- *Mothers-in-law interfere.*
- *Mothers-in-law are critical.*
- *Mothers-in-law are not good for a marriage.*
- *Mothers-in-law are bossy.*
- *Mothers-in-law are competitive.*
- *Mothers-in-law are only good for babysitting.*
- *Mothers-in-law think their daughters-in-law/sons-in-law are not good enough for their sons/daughters.*
- *Mothers-in-law are takers, not givers.*
- *Mothers-in-law expect perfection.*
- *Mothers-in-law should always be strangers.*

Wait a minute! What's wrong with this picture? Did someone forget that all mothers-in-law are *mothers* first? Okay, nobody's perfect. And few mothers-in-law ever get labeled as saints. But please, let's remember that we're dealing with human beings here. Mom doesn't automatically become a critical, competitive buttinsky just because one of her children got married!

...and Almost-Perfect Mothers-in-Law

You didn't cause the problem, but — for better or for worse — it's up to you to fix it.

The mother-in-law must take the initiative in breaking the stereotypes. She is, after all, the mature member and natural leader of the "in-law family." She can set the tone, and be the model, for a healthy and positive relationship.

Perhaps you're thinking, "I can say that. I have every right to express my opinion. After all, it's my daughter (son)." Yes, you can say whatever you want, and you do have the right, but if you want to maintain a close relationship with your child and his/her spouse, you'd best not.

Permit me to suggest instead for your consideration three rules of sensible (and loving) conduct:

Find the Right words: Lots of things mothers-in-law say are valid, the information correct and useful. The trouble is, *no one wants to be told what to do.* It may be that, when a mother-in-law speaks, children hear a mother giving orders, treating them as if they were little girls or boys, while they are still fighting for independence. Remember how your two-year old screamed, "Me do it!" and how, in adolescence, the battle for independence was renewed when your teenager rebelliously announced, "Don't tell me what to do!" The fear of lost independence never disappears. You need to realize that *any* advice you can offer may be heard by others as dominating criticism: "I'm only trying to help" comes across to your in-law children as "I don't think you are capable."

To avoid conflict, better *offer an opinion only when asked,* and then with much forethought. For example, when consulted about decorating problems, try, "If I were setting up this room, I think I'd try the blue sofa against that wall. It would make a comfortable seating arrangement, and I wouldn't have to think about whether it's going to fade or not. What do you think?" or "Here's what I did when I set up our home. Maybe the same arrangement could work for you." Avoid a directive, "Here's where the sofa goes!" or a critical, "Why did you put the sofa there? The sun will hit it and the fabric will disintegrate. It cost a fortune, and you'll have to replace it in no time!" Such spontaneous "suggestions" are sure to be taken as meddling or interference by your adult children.

(You may even find that the youngsters will avoid an obviously "best" selection *just because* you suggested it.)

The best avenue to being helpful is to *allow your adult children to figure it out for themselves.* Ask leading questions, reflect what you hear them say, help them focus their thoughts. Remember that *they* have to live with their decisions. You don't.

If you don't nurture a relationship — child, in-law or any other — it disappears; you lose the connection. You certainly don't want to do that with your children; so you must work at your new in-law relationship. Find a balance, know when to take the back seat (without trying to drive from there), and understand that expressing feelings and ideas requires much thought — and some finely honed verbal skills. (Chapter Six takes an in-depth look at issues in family communication.)

Bridget, a mother of six, told me, "We're a large, noisy, Irish family, especially when it comes to politics. We love a loud discussion — a friendly, spirited debate, not an angry thing. Others who sit in and hear our arguments sometimes become fearful because of the intensity of the controversy.

"I began to sense my daughter-in-law, Elizabeth, was cowed. She comes from a family of quiet people who don't argue — an ultra-liberal family — and my children romp all over her with 'What do you mean?' when she offers freethinking ideas. People who are not used to debating are put off by it, and Elizabeth was truly intimidated.

"Like most Irish debaters," Bridget says matter-of-factly, "I can see both sides of a story. My husband used to say, 'You're like a Philadelphia lawyer.' My children would line up the arguments against Elizabeth, and I'd feel bad because she'd be overwhelmed and fold quickly. I began to see that wasn't going well for her, so I decided to weigh-in — gently — to help Elizabeth mount her arguments."

She laughed, "I gave her ammunition so she could hold her own, and told the other kids, 'We have to take it a bit easy, learn to modify our exhuberance.'

"People think if you argue with someone you have to be angry," Bridget said, "but it's not true. In our family it's like playing a game of chess. You don't get upset when you're not a winner. You enjoy the game — and there's always the possibility you might convince the other to see your side."

Bridget had real concern for her daughter-in-law. Aware of the younger woman's anxiety, she was able to switch sides even though her beliefs were different. Evaluating the situation, she asked herself, "What's important here?" Her need wasn't to be right but to make her daughter-in-law more comfortable.

It's easy to forget that the conditions that formed our in-law children were very different from those in our own families, and consequently, they have dissimilar ideas. That doesn't mean you can't have a close relationship with them, no matter what their political, social or religious beliefs. What you have to do is get past your expectations, political or otherwise, and talk together. In order to have an escape valve, sometimes it's okay to *say* you don't need to see eye to eye.

Bridget had real concern for her daughter-in-law. Aware of the younger woman's anxiety, she was able to switch sides even though her beliefs were different. Evaluating the situation, she asked herself, "What's important here?" Her need wasn't to be right but to make her daughter-in-law more comfortable.

Don't Impose: As parents, we believe we're saving our adult children time and extra work by doing for them things that they could do for themselves, but this irks them to tears. In fact, it builds hostility. They see these efforts as an infringement on their independence — a takeover attempt. And maybe you *are* holding on to them too tightly. If it's not your problem, it's best *not* to say *anything*.

Let me emphasize it again: *offer advice only when asked, and then, very gently.* Recall when you were a new bride; then you'll understand. Besides, you don't want a power struggle, so the best thing is to back away, to let your kids stand on their own feet, to give your adult children space.

My own mother, when I first married, wanted a key to our apartment. "In case I'm in the neighborhood," she said, "and have to go to the bathroom." I resented her asking, my husband more so, and although I felt uncomfortable saying no, I did. I didn't care what *she* wanted; I only knew what I wanted. Selfish? I don't think so. My husband and I were creating a new life for ourselves, and we didn't need an uninvited guest.

Thirty-five years later, I can still recall how intrusive her request felt. It was my home, and her demand was an infringement on my privacy. Even close friends and family don't ask for keys. They call first before they visit; they don't pop in unannounced. And certainly not when we're not at home.

I would have been pleased if my own mother'd had some of Bridget's sensitivity, but every parent, like every child, is different.

My son and daughter, on the other hand, each have keys to my home. I tell them, "This house is your house. You're always welcome — come whenever you want." The difference is that, as a new bride, I was still battling for separation. Because I was immature, anything my mother or mother-in-law said smacked of control, even when that wasn't the case. It was important to me to prove that I was a responsible adult who could run her own life.

Today, I'm not afraid of losing my privacy, or that my children will judge my housekeeping. I don't feel threatened anymore, because I know who I am. But that has taken years.

Encourage Integrity: In addition to knowing who you are, it's important to be *authentic* with your adult children. That includes exposing them to your negative feelings as well as positive ones.

It's truly difficult at times to talk openly to a daughter- or son-in-law, to express how you feel, openly, firmly but kindly. And it's especially hard for those of us who were "good" girls as youngsters, taught to hide feelings, to keep opinion to ourselves. It can be painful to reveal yourself. But if you aren't honest, what can you expect from them? *You set the stage* — for a real relationship, or a phony one.

Take a look at your own behavior: the way *you* act has consequences!

You can make good as well as bad things happen. A mother-in-law has to learn that — sometimes the hard way. It's easy to consider yourself a victim, but when you do, you're also handing over responsibility for what occurs in your life. Instead of getting rid of the chip on your shoulder, and connecting the negative consequences directly to your own actions, you blame others. Time to grow up, isn't it?

You probably don't take credit for the nice things that happen in your life either. Perhaps you say instead, "I was just lucky," or "My son/daughter-in-law was in a good mood today."

Take Elena, who knows her son-in-law doesn't speak Greek. "Shortly after we were married," Jeff said, "she made a fancy dinner party for us at an upscale restaurant, inviting many relatives and friends. Calliope, a cousin, insisted on speaking Greek, and my mother-in-law at first answered in her native tongue, but she smoothly shifted into English," Jeff observed, "so I could understand what was going on. Elena's extremely considerate. She has a phenomenal sense of grace and hospitality."

Elena also has the ability to make wise decisions and probably takes credit for the good things that happen in her life.

The truth is, if we weren't such hard taskmasters, we would recognize how competent we mothers-in-law are and tell ourselves, "I made some good decisions!"

Our adult children, too, often don't make connections about their behavior and blame others. It may be easier for them to fight through issues with a mother-in-law than to work them out with the appropriate person. "Human nature," Judith Viorst tells us in *Necessary Losses*, "has a compulsion to repeat. . . . Thus whom we love and how we love are revivals — unconscious — of earlier experiences, even when revival brings pain. We act out the same tragedies unless awareness and insight intervenes."

Irene grew up feeling insecure and jealous of females in her family because her own mother was competitive. Her mother saw Irene as a rival, but not her brothers. As males, they were not a threat. Now Irene grows up, marries, has sons of her own and, inevitably, a daughter-in-law. Irene will very likely treat the daughter-in-law the same way her mother treated her.

Felice Toonkel, a New Jersey psychoanalyst offers this view, "In the original scenario she couldn't work her feelings out, and here, once again, is another competitive female like mother.

"Consciously, the mother-in-law says, 'I want to have a good relationship with my daughter-in-law,' but at an unconscious level she's afraid the daughter-in-law will take her son away. At the bottom of this is fear. In short, the mother-in-law fears she will lose her son, and has a need to protect herself. But if she can grow, a mother-in-law will understand the dilemma of her early life and be able to work through it, learning to be gently assertive. If she doesn't she will repeat it — acting out, trying to get her needs met."

So how do you know if you're acting on feelings that have nothing to do with the present? "Ask yourself," Ms. Toonkel advises, "Have these feelings happened to me before? Have I felt jealousy, rage, or being used another time in my life?'"

When your emotions are intense, what you want to do is *not act*. Stop! Wait until you can behave in the best possible way. This is a time when counting to ten is so important.

Becoming Yourself

It takes decades to grow up. Perhaps, now that your children are moving away, you are at the right moment to become a wise woman. Moreover, you should know that if you seek to separate from parents, dead or alive, the process won't be easy. You have a struggle to undertake. It's quite an effort to find out who you really are. But the rewards are usually worth it. If you can get in touch with your fears and angers and become honest with yourself, you can be honest with your children.

Only when you can admit your foibles can you eradicate your own perfection myths. Then you may accept that we are all human and make mistakes. Only then can you really love.

"It doesn't happen all at once" says the *The Velveteen Rabbit's* wise nursery friend, the Skin Horse. "You become. It takes a long time. That's why it doesn't often happen to people who break easily, or have sharp edges, or who have to be carefully kept. Generally by the time you are Real, most of your hair has been loved off, and your eyes drop out and you get loose in the joints and very shabby. But these things don't matter at all, because once you are Real you can't be ugly, except to people who don't understand... but once you are Real you can't become unreal again. It lasts for always."

Your son and daughter-in-law are in college, and live in your city. Both are working part-time while they're in school, and they have very little time for anything else. You've visited their apartment a few times, and it's always a mess. You want desperately to help out. You decide to:
  a. Offer to stop by once a week and "straighten up the place."
  b. Give them a gift certificate for a cleaning service.
  c. Suggest that they'd be more comfortable and more efficient if they'd clean house once in a while.
  d. Take your daughter-in-law aside and let her know that your son is used to living in a clean house.
  e. Take your son aside and remind him that these days men can clean house too.
  f. Buy them a vacuum cleaner for their anniversary.
  g. Hold your tongue and close your eyes to the mess.

What's likely to result from each action?
  a. Would you have wanted your mother or mother-in-law to clean your house when you were a newlywed?
  b. Have they wished aloud for help with the cleaning?
  c. This is a value judgement they may not share.
  d. What will you say if she answers, "If it's important to him, he can clean it!"?
  e. A healthy idea you probably should have taught him years ago.
  f. One more item to clutter up the place. Have they asked for one?
  g. Probably your best choice, if you can handle it.

Chapter 2

QUILTS, SCRIPTS, AND SCAPEGOATS:
Becoming "the Other Mother"

*T*hink of your family as a patchwork quilt.

Each person is a unique piece of the quilt, and each piece is formed to interlock with the others and to fit into a specific space. As a growing child, you fill the space created for you in your family quilt. In most families, that space is lovingly fitted — trimmed or stretched as needed — into the total design.

Later, when you marry, you add another person to the design. The inclusion of your spouse represents a time of readjustment, a chance to reshape the patchwork pieces so they once again fit and interconnect perfectly, in a healthy way. And along with your spouse you have to incorporate his family members — your in-laws — into the artwork. The two family quilts may not fit smoothly together. One quilt's pieces may have pointed corners; the other's curved edges. Whatever the original configurations, the challenge will be to bring the two quilts together, despite the gaps and rough edges.

When your children grow up and marry, their spouses, the in-law children, also will become part of the quilt — members of your family. And they bring with them their own family quilts.

The edges of their pieces may seem to you to be rough; their needs, hopes, desires, values and traditions not at all like yours. They are, in short, different.

But "different" doesn't mean bad, or inferior, or less valuable — just *different*. They came from another place. Their quilt pieces have been shaped by their own unique traditions, values, environments, experiences.

As each new piece is connected to your quilt, there will be changes. You'll have to let go of the way things used to be. This process may take months if you are lucky, but it could be years before everybody is able to adapt and connect.

The important thing is that the borders of your family quilt must be flexible enough to   accommodate such changes. Transitions are constant. There must be flexibility and tolerance in order to meet everyone's needs — to finally have the quilt come out "right."

During our lifetimes we redo our family quilts with variations over and over again. We keep trying to resolve the discord of the past, and to accommodate the changes that come as the family grows and shrinks. We're trying, constantly, to get all the pieces to fit perfectly.

Most of us, when we marry, choose a person who meets many of our unmet needs, someone with whom we can work out our original "unfinished business" from the past. The process of falling in love and choosing a life partner is complex and, unlike the movies, things don't always go well. Most of us don't want to face the loss of the "happily-ever-after" myth, of course. We cling to the notion that he or she will make everything perfect, keep us comfortable, and provide for all our needs. Oftentimes, we can't even admit that we have a problem, so we look for a scapegoat. When the quilt pieces don't mesh properly, the tendency is to shift the disappointment to a third party. And, alas, that third party is often — guess who? — the mother-in-law.

Family Scripts

Let's once again admit that *no one is perfect*. We've all been raised by less-than-perfect parents and have had imperfect childhoods. Our desires weren't fulfilled perfectly every time, we were left with *unmet needs*. Typical results of all this imperfection: jealousy, envy, a poor self-image, low frustration tolerance, anger, fear, and rivalry.

Young children learn who they are from their parents. They are "formatted" by a combination of genetic predispositions and early life experiences — both of which come from their parents.

Early on, as young as five or six, our child incorporates into his psyche a set of instructions for the way he will react to any social or psychological situation he encounters for the rest of his life. He learns to favor the kind of food his parents eat, to speak in the tones of voice he hears us use, to value what we value, discard what we don't like. He learns our roles, our wants, our reactions, how we cope, what methods we use to get our needs met, what we touch, what we feel, how we play, how we love, how we hate.

As he grows and matures, and experiences new people and events, the child's early behavioral patterns adapt and change. He has the ability to make choices, to alter, accept, or reject what doesn't feel good or doesn't produce the results he needs. Some patterns will be modified by outside influences, but generally, in his adult life, a child will repeat the patterns of the past because they are well known and familiar. It doesn't matter whether they have been constructive or unhealthy. Even if these patterns have been most uncomfortable, they taught him what he needed to do and be, and how to keep his parents involved with him so that he could survive in that family.

Eventually, the child becomes an adult, a survivor. His next step is to choose a life partner — and begin to create his own new section of the family quilt. The traditional ritual that symbolizes that step toward independence is the same one that makes you a mother-in-law: his wedding.

"I Now Pronounce You..."

Weddings are a big step in growing up, not only for our children but for us parents — the in-laws — as well.

Although they're happy occasions, you have to assume that things may not run smoothly. Differences frequently arise because weddings are a time of high emotion, and there are so many personalities to satisfy, each with a different set of values. When uncomfortable feelings kick in, many in-laws take a path of least resistance. Feelings make us uncomfortable, so we shove them under the rug, but they don't disappear. The human memory is a powerful device!

The mother of the groom may find the wedding a particularly difficult time. In most American family traditions, the groom's mother is an unequal partner in the wedding plans. From day one, she has to learn to adapt, to take a step back, and to put things in perspective so she won't jeopardize future relationships. She gets an early start on one key rule for a mother-in-law: to refrain from saying anything that may come back to haunt her — or her son — later.

The truly valiant among us try to minimize differences and aim for a win-win situation, so that all involved parties may have their needs met. None of us are the same (that's what makes life interesting), but *no one* wants to hear a new daughter- or son-in-law say, "My mother-in-law spoiled my wedding."

Weddings can be an ideal opportunity to begin practicing for your lifelong job as mother-in-law. The name of the game now is *acceptance*. While some daughters/sons-in-law are easier to love than others, *we must all accept the choice our children make,* and welcome these new members into our families.

Do you really want to learn how to do that? Do you have to? You bet. After years of being able to say whatever you please with friends and trusted family members, you now have to watch your words.

The Wedding Is Only the Beginning

Wedding bells signify not only a time of euphoria, but also an emotional ripping away. People are pulled at before weddings, and lots of "shoulds" (beliefs of what you and others have to do) come into play. "Shoulds" stem from the way you were raised — your environment and cultural background.

Psychotherapist Felice Toonkel points out, "This is the time parents have to wrestle with abandonment issues they may never have examined before. Mothers-in-law have to realize marriage is a big separation issue for the family, and it has to be dealt with as much as women need to deal with menopause. It is an issue of loss, perhaps more significant than the empty-nest syndrome issue, when a child leaves home to go to college. At that time, the child returns for holidays and vacations, still visiting back and forth, and generally includes parents in decision making."

It's a long process of work to relinquish control. We need to be ready for compromise and tolerance. And most importantly, we must remember *we can only change ourselves.* Each human being owns his or her own emotional reality, and you cannot force yours on another.

Respect is the operative word here. We all have to pause for a moment and think before acting, to be respectful of each other's needs. You don't want to become a divisive force in this new complex relationship. Among the challenges: to give up thinking of the young couple as an extension of yourself, and not to blame the in-law child or the other set of parents for everything that goes wrong.

Most in-laws are predisposed to act kindly. But as we have seen, early learning dies hard. Some of us are driven to repeat our relationships with our own in-laws, while others go to great lengths to avoid it. Either extreme can cause havoc. Mothers-in-law who have been competitive with their own mothers in the past, for example, may close themselves off from a healthy relationship with their children unless they examine their actions and get to know themselves, the *real* person beneath the facade.

Ideally, you should review your own history, the connections you had with your parents, and your own family scripts. Did your parents expect you to do whatever they told you to do? If you didn't have permission to make decisions when you were a youngster, you may have a great deal of trouble allowing your adult children to make their own choices.

The First Year of Marriage

The first year of a marriage is a difficult time for most newlyweds. There are many issues that arise that the young couple must confront. Not the least of those are the very complex relationships with their respective parents/in-laws.

A mother-in-law who, for instance, had a better relationship with her son than she had with her husband may easily make trouble in her child's marriage. She may, perhaps unconsciously, want to hold on to her son; she has another agenda for him. To her, a daughter-in-law is an infringement on her territory, and becomes "triangled" into the mother-son relationship. Inevitably there will be conflict. A daughter-in-law with a healthy ego of her own may not be threatened. However, if she's a bit insecure, or has unresolved problems with her own mother, she may over-react. She may lay old feelings of resentment onto her mother-in-law, find fault at every opportunity, and guard her husband jealously.

Let's look in on a few common early-marriage scenes. Do you recognize yourself in any of them?

Scene One

Amy (Wife): "You never take me anywhere."

Michael (Husband): "We can't go out and leave the house like this. The place is a mess. Everything's upside down. It looks like a bomb exploded here."

Amy (cries): "Well, I can't do everything!"

Michael: "All right, all right. Get dressed! We'll go to a movie."

When Amy was a child her mother yelled, "Look at the room! It's a mess! You're a mess! Look at your hair. Don't you care about yourself?" The child cried, so mother, now feeling guilty, hugged her, saying , "Don't cry. I was planning to go to the craft fair, but this room needs to be cleaned, so I'll stay home and clean it. You know I love you."

As a child, Amy learned that in order to get love you have to take criticism, but if you cry, you are loved and get your needs met. She has learned how to manipulate through tears. As an adult, she will likely continue to manipulate people by crying. After that, criticism will follow from parent, spouse, or friend — and this will lead to reassurance and, eventually, to love. So when her mother-in-law visits and reacts to the mess in her house, saying, "You must have been busy this week. I see you didn't get a chance to clean. Why don't the two of you go out and I'll take care of it," this daughter-in-law won't laugh it off. Instead, she'll feel insulted and ashamed; here come those old feelings from childhood! She'll burst into tears or explode angrily to her husband, "Your mother drives me crazy, she makes me feel so inadequate!"

Now she has made her mother-in-law the scapegoat for her feelings, and set up her husband to be her rescuer. Michael is expected to play out the old role. He may have his own problems, but he gets caught in the middle; his loyalty is both to his wife and to his mother. Nevertheless, he is expected — by social custom — to defend and rescue his wife. Amy, in turn, hopes her mother-in-law will come to love her and accept her the same way her mother did.

Mother-in-law, meanwhile, has no clue to what's going on! Besides, she has her own upbringing to deal with. Though she is trying to be helpful, the message to her daughter-in-law is, "I disapprove of the way you keep house. Your house is dirty." To have a good relationship with the newlyweds, this mother-in-law needs to hold her tongue and not volunteer to do anything unless asked.

The rule is clear: if you, mother-in-law, see the dishes piled in the sink and the grease on the stove thick enough to write your name in — *look away*. Cleaning up is passing judgement. Instead, treat your daughter-in-law as if she were a friend inviting you for tea. Tell yourself, "This is not my house. It's not my place to clean it," and concentrate on strengthening the relationship with your children.

Later, when you've established a close relationship, perhaps after a few years, your daughter-in-law *may* be comfortable if you intervene gently. If you find her rushing about during your visit, trying to balance career and domestic chores — and possibly a child — you might tactfully comment, "I'd be glad to help if there's anything I can do. I know you're carrying quite a load these days."

Scene Two

Mother: "Daddy and I are going out tonight. I know we planned to be together, Amy, but something came up. Tomorrow we'll go shopping, and you can pick any present you like."

Child (cries): "But you promised!"

Father: "We don't have to go."

Mother: "We're going! I told Martha we'd be there."

This scene takes place again and again, and Amy learns that:

- She's not important
- Gifts are a substitute for people
- Gifts mean love
- Amy's needs don't count
- Women have power

When Amy marries, her needs will come first. If her husband has to work late, she will complain, "Your job is more important to you than I am," and will resent any time her husband spends with his family, especially with his mother-in-law. Amy wants all her husband's attention. No matter how nice this mother-in-law is, she will rub her daughter-in-law the wrong way. Amy unconsciously sees her mother-in-law as *another* ungiving mother.

Scene Three

Here's a different situation where the problem has been deflected onto the mother-in-law. Suppose that one Saturday morning Amy's mother-in-law, a widow, calls and asks her son for help with stuck windows. Her apartment has just been painted. This is what follows:

Michael: "I'll be glad to help, Mom."

Amy (angrily): "I've worked all week. There's so much to do around here. You can't go! She can wait!"

Amy has an irrational response to her mother-in-law's request. She feels undervalued; is unreasonably jealous, and her husband is confused because his mother rarely asks for anything. Michael doesn't understand what's happening — why his wife is reacting this way. He doesn't realize his mother has become the replacement for Amy's ungiving mother. He doesn't recognize the power of her early scripts.

Let's take this scene one step further. If Michael leaves to help his mother, Amy might repeat another old pattern: to go shopping, binge impulsively, buy whatever tempts her, spend too much money, and give herself the presents her mother gave her as a child.

This mother-in-law will have to bend over backwards to have a good relationship with her daughter-in-law. If the two women can talk honestly, and Amy can tell her mother-in-law that she upset her plans for the day, it's a step in the right direction. But this mother-in-law will have to listen very, very carefully to be able to accurately read the signals, and she'll have to keep a lid on her own jealousy and resentment. It's difficult to forgive when you are hurt because you want to nurture your own wounds, so this will be a formidable task. Many mothers-in-law would go on the defensive, responding with, "I didn't do anything wrong!"

But if Amy's mother-in-law is smart, and if she wants a relationship with her daughter-in-law, the antidote would be to say, "I feel really bad this misunderstanding occurred. What can I do to avoid the problem in the future?"

Holiday Celebrations and Other Expectations

During initial marital adjustments, it's normal for many changes to occur in families. In-laws and adult children have needs and expectations of each other, and conflicts do arise. It's important to make sure that these don't gouge out pieces of your heart or become unmanageable resentment.

Let's examine a situation where a daughter-in-law — Janet — has a high-powered career and lives close to her husband's family. The mother-in-law — Carol — believes that all the holidays should be celebrated at her house. That is the way Carol's mother celebrated the holidays when she was newly married, and she is repeating the role. Carol thinks that she's making life easier for her children. She is, after all, an excellent cook who loves having her family around.

But Janet doesn't want to make a fuss about holidays. For her they are a time to be alone with her husband (Sam) — perhaps to go away for a few days. And because the women have never talked about their needs with each other, especially those regarding holiday observances, there is a potentially dangerous lack of understanding. Only disappointments and bad feelings can follow, and Sam feels as if he is being pulled apart.

In this drama each person's expectations have to change. But whose problem is it? If the mother-in-law is unhappy, it's her problem, and she has to do something about it. It would be ideal if both women learned to give a little, but if not, Carol, who wants a good relationship with her children, will have to take the initial step, become flexible, and accept her daughter-in-law with her differences.

This mother-in-law has to step out of herself. She has to learn to empathize with Janet's needs and desires. She may even have to give up her expectations about what people do on holidays. If Carol sees the problem as a shared issue and tries for a win-win solution, Sam and Janet may want to fulfill her needs at another time or in another way. If she holds on too tightly, pressuring them, the young couple will likely pull away.

Becoming "The Other Mother"

Sometimes a daughter-in-law will expect her mother-in-law to be better than the mother she had, to make up for the losses in her childhood. If the mother-in-law comes through, she will have a daughter-in-law who will idolize her. If the daughter-in-law expects her husband's mother to be as lousy as her own mother, however, she may never give you a chance. What can one do?

You can focus on trying to build a good relationship — to be a *friendly other*. Convey a sense of caring but don't come on too strong. People with poor self-images are super-sensitive, so learn to listen, to be accepting, to really hear what your daughter-in-law is saying. (Chapter 6 offers some help with communication skills.) You have to know when to stay silent, and when to be supportive. Look for things to like, and be as positive as you can.

Consider the reverse situation: if you had poor parenting yourself, how can you expect to become a good mother-in-law? If you feel lonely and crave attention, when you are with your grown children you may act like a dependent child. Instead of forming a network of peer-friends of your own, you may be calling your child constantly, visiting every week, leaning on the newlyweds, always having an agenda. Your over-involvement may meet some of your needs for contact and affirmation, but it's likely pushing your children away emotionally.

Take Jean for example. After years of being important, she feels she has lost her value and her source of self esteem — her *raison d'etre*. Jean may be the sort of woman who has spent her life as a homemaker and no longer knows what to do with herself. All of a sudden her days are never ending. Jean has too much time on her hands and — as we all find out sooner or later — being a mother-in-law, even a good one, isn't much of a role.

You don't have to be a clinging vine. If you resemble one, here's what you can do. First, you have to *stop feeling sorry for yourself* and talk about your lack of a role, possibly with a friend, perhaps with a therapist. Look beyond your children to build self-esteem. Next, you have to *step back,* because you may have a tendency to do too much for the kids, and you are not helping them to grow. Finally, you have to change, to make a plan to *build a life for yourself.*

Young couples want privacy for themselves, and a needy person is not fun to be with. When someone leans on you, the tendency is to pull away. A mother-in-law might adopt the role, "Poor me! My children don't care if I live or die." To prove herself right, she plays out the script, "Didn't I tell you, a son is a son until he takes a wife. . . ." This mother-in-law could easily set in motion a self-fulfilling prophecy. She has never accepted the fact that her children are adults and that she has to take a back seat; there has been a rearrangement of lives.

When you move furniture from one place to another, things don't always seem to fit immediately. Some circumstances need to grow on you. There are people, however, who don't lend themselves to adjustments; they fight change and keep wanting to reinstate the status quo. When her children are no longer living at home, a mother has to look at her lack of a role and think about what she does with her time and then change her patterns. Find ways of fulfilling her needs that do not depend on her children. One step would be to develop a network of friends.

"Bug Off, Mom!"

Now let's look at another family triangle. In this situation, mother-in-law Doris wants to prove that her son Al loves her as much as his new wife, Elena. An authoritarian mother all her life,

Doris is used to controlling everything around her, and is not fond of compromise. She has to be the boss, and is always right; there is no negotiating. Al is used to obeying his mother, and even though the umbilical cord was cut at birth, Doris still doesn't believe it. If Al can't buck his mother, and continues to put her wishes ahead of Elena's, as Doris expects, eventually his marriage may be destroyed.

The sword has two edges, of course: If Al *is* able to handle his mother, Doris will blame her daughter-in-law. Now that he's married, for example, Al doesn't call his mother every day. Doris's response script is written this way: "I could have died," she whines, "and you wouldn't even have known it."

This adult temper tantrum makes demands that push other people away. Not only that, as Doris will discover, it creates more tension. Al feels angry, and Elena feels intruded upon. In some families this is handled by the daughter-in-law, who becomes the mouthpiece for the son. If she's very nice, when her mother-in-law calls she may say "I know it's disappointing when Al doesn't phone you, but he's been working overtime, and you have to understand."

A not-so-nice — perhaps resentful — daughter-in-law may shout, "Bug off, Doris! Leave us alone!"

Every mother-in-law needs straight talk from her children. A mature person will let go of unrealistic expectations. Being immature, Doris has to learn that the old ways are no longer relevant, that her son is not going to report in to her every day, and that, if they don't speak, it doesn't mean he doesn't love her. By being less aggressive, Doris will, in fact, have a better relationship with her children. The most important thing for Doris to realize is that she must back off, give these newlyweds space. If she's the one who calls, because she needs the contact, she must learn to make her chat fast and friendly.

The Role of a Mother-In-Law

The role of a mother-in-law is to help her children feel secure. To be loved by her married children, she cannot just be a "nice lady." It doesn't work that way; good things don't "just happen." As in parenting, a mother-in-law has to work at the relationship and give more than half. It may take a lot of wooing to be accepted by in-law children.

The mother-in-law has advantages, of course. Age and experience are on her side. She knows the past in the present. She may be able to predict consequences from behaviors, foresee a vision of the future. Certainly she knows what it feels like to be where her son/daughter-in-law is today. She has observed "triangles" — scapegoating the "odd-man-out" — played out with friends, nieces and nephews. She's even had practice wearing the same hat as her in-law child. And she is, after all, the more mature member of the triangle. She should be able to avoid some of the hazards.

It's true that some daughters/sons-in-law are easier to love than others, but it's up to each of us to accept the choice our child has made, no matter what. Most of us truly want to incorporate this in-law child into our family. We want to say "I haven't lost a child, I've gained one." If we act on this belief, we can make it a reality.

You'll see that it is in your power to change thoughts in your head, be *authentically* "nice" and effect a difference in feelings, which in turn will help you avoid daughter/son-in-law trouble. If she doesn't change negative thoughts, a mother-in-law can sabotage her relationship with her children, and perhaps their marriage as well. We don't want to lose our children, and we don't want to undermine their lives. The truth is, as we get older we need them more than they need us. We simply have to be wiser.

It's not easy to switch from being a mother to an in-law parent, or to give up trying to be the ultimate authority in our children's lives, even when they're adults. In reality, like it or not, our adult children are in charge of their own lives. As their centers of interest shift, loyalties shift, and in-law parents have to deal with separation and change. Tension and anxiety may grow; therefore, you must be open to examining your life, ready for new ideas, and be able to establish a different niche for yourself.

You can build on your experience; you've been a nurturer for many years. As a mother-in-law, you can try to understand the newlyweds and be less judgmental. When you express love, you teach others to express it. And amazingly, through loving others, we all learn that we are worth loving, too. We discover the strengths we teach others to find.

Prepare Yourself

You probably feel intimidated tackling a daughter or son-in-law, trying to improve a not-so-wonderful relationship because it provokes so much apprehension. However, if you handle each problem as it arises, the feelings won't intensify. You might want to try *visual imaging*.

To do this, sit in a comfortable chair, close your eyes, and take a few deep breaths. Now relax. Envision a happy scene. Conjure up a picture of yourself talking easily to your son or daughter-in-law. Say what you have to, clearly, smoothly, gently, kindly. Hear the conversation going well, the words flowing. Imagine yourself getting your needs met. Let yourself feel the good feelings — love and affection. Hold on to them. Dream the scene again and again at different times during the day, for a week, for two. Practice saying what you want out loud. If you do this, you will have a greater chance of resolving your problem, because you've rehearsed it. It's what Olympic athletes do before a meet. Imaging is how they psych themselves up to win. They get their adrenaline flowing, pumping themselves up, seeing their moment of triumph when they surge across the finish line a winner.

Letting Go... and Finding Yourself

Instead of working on our conflicts, too many of us want to wish them away, to deny that they even exist. It takes courage to move ahead, to challenge the unknown. If you close your eyes to your problems, you can't let them go.

At such times a person who is healthy and vigorous may even develop physical symptoms rather than deal with strife. Many times people don't even make the connection that the physical problem is really caused by an emotional problem. It's the only way some people have of expressing the conflicts within. The mind and the body can't be separated.

It takes a long time to let go of the messages you've collected through the years, even the self-destructive ones. Some people may never rid themselves of having an agenda for others, trying to remake relationships to suit themselves. They stay with the old patterns and never change. Furthermore, many don't even recognize what is happening. But if you can mature to know who *you* are, the *real* person within, with all your imperfections, and can forgive them, what follows is that you grow to love yourself. It will give you understanding of what relationships are all about.

Your daughter and son-in-law have decided to move to the city, several hundred miles from your home. They're convinced that their careers will be enhanced by taking jobs in big companies, and that means going where the jobs are. You're concerned about crime, pollution, schools for your grandchildren, and the likelihood that visits will be less frequent. You decide to:

    a. Offer to buy them a home in your town if they'll stay.
    b. Offer them jobs in your company.
    c. Pass along lots of statistics about the dangers of city life.
    d. Investigate the city schools and share with them what you learn.
    e. Call their current bosses and plead for raises to keep them here.
    f. Invite them to dinner and ask them to tell you about their goals and plans.
    g. Say nothing and hope for the best (maybe they won't get jobs).

What's your best guess about the outcomes here?

    a. Don't you think there might be just a bit of resentment from this heavy-handed move?
    b. If you have a company, they must surely have considered the possibility. Did they apply?
    c. If this idea is appealing, be sure you include lots of statistics about the advantages of city life as well.
    d. If your presentation is balanced, this could be useful.
    e. Hey, Mrs. Buttinsky, here you go again!
    f. I like this one. Keep the lines of communication open.
    g. Pretty wimpy, don't you think? If you care, say so.

Chapter 3

WHOSE DREAMS?
The Other Mother Chronicles

*W*hen our children are young, we give them years of our lives — the best years, the young years, the good years. We pass along traditions that are familiar, and often our unfulfilled expectations for ourselves as well. Everything we lacked growing up, we usually want for our children. For example, I wanted *my* son and daughter to have a better education and the ability to travel. I hoped they would speak several languages, play musical instruments, and be well informed and unafraid. Everything I was not, I needed them to be, and when they matured and achieved many of the goals I set for them, I found it hard to relinquish control of these adult children.

But our children are not our possessions. They belong to themselves. They are on loan to us for only a short while, and when they mature, we must surrender to the inevitable and let go. They must separate to be whole people. That is when we have to face our losses, adapt, and weed out all the expectations we had for them.

If your children are healthy and have a strong self-image, they will be able to make plans for themselves and have their own expectations about what *they* would like to have happen in their future. They will have goals. Hopes. Plans. Wishes. Fantasies.

But some mothers-in-law (and mothers) may not want to relinquish their expectations for their children, expectations that perhaps include themselves — dreams where anything wonderful is possible, and make-believe can come true.

Unrealistic expectations may have been shaped by fears of abandonment or other left-over needs from your childhood; goals that you didn't achieve when you were younger and now, as you grow older, you are still trying to fill. Unfortunately this often leads to living vicariously through married children.

Not realizing it, you are asking your children to grant these wishes, make up for disappointments. In effect, you are hoping they will make *your* dreams come true, repair some damage that happened years ago. So you make plans for your son and daughter-in-law and your daughter and son-in-law, but they let you know that you are out of sync with their needs.

Your expectations are not applauded: They don't please your children. They antagonize and frustrate them, complicating your relationships. The acceptance that you strive for is replaced with rejection, because you are too ambitious.

Take Meryl, for example. As a young mother, she focused on her career, and she thinks her relationship with her son Tim has suffered because of it. Now that Tim is grown and married, Meryl feels a deep sense of loss, because she wasn't always available when he needed her. Meryl regrets that she missed the everyday nurturing opportunities for loving exchanges, and says to her daughter-in-law, "Your top priority, Cathleen, should be your husband and the children, or else you'll miss out on their day-to-day growth. You don't need a full-time career. Tim makes a good living. Why don't you just take a part-time job?"

This is advice-giving without considering the needs of the younger woman. It's telling Cathleen how to live. It will not endear Meryl to her daughter-in-law.

If she wants to have a rapport with the younger woman, she might try to share a part of herself instead. "I've had a wonderful career," she could say, "but I have many regrets, too. One is putting my job ahead of my son. I was forever juggling my business needs with Tim's schedule, and not enjoying him as much as I could have. Always waiting for Tim to grow up. Looking back, I'm sorry. I realize now that time goes too fast, and every day is special."

Now let's look at Paula, a hard-working speech therapist. Her son-in-law, Matthew, is a musician in a band, hoping one day to be a major rock star. Paula is fearful for her daughter's future, worried about the financial aspects of the marriage. There is some validity in her concern, too; Matthew doesn't earn enough to support them.

Paula's father was financially unsuccessful. He also had artistic aspirations. She, her siblings, and mother lived from hand to mouth, and Paula doesn't want the same for her daughter. Paula is married to a corporate lawyer who works sixteen-hour days but has no time for his family, though he does provide every luxury the family desires. Paula wants her daughter to have the lifestyle she knows, not the one her grandparents had. But the girl has chosen Matthew. Maybe it's a reaction to her upbringing. Maybe she wanted a male figure who was available at all times, someone who showed her that *she*, rather than money, mattered.

Paula is constantly telling her son-in-law, "The odds of making it in the music industry are very slim. You ought to hedge your bets, go back to school, and get a degree in something practical. Have your music as a hobby!"

If Paula opened her eyes, she'd see that her unsolicited advice makes Matthew uneasy and her daughter angry. Matthew considers Paula a meddling mother-in-law, and resents her interference.

By judging her children's lifestyle, Paula is telling them that they're incapable of taking care of their future. She has to learn that she can't plan for her children; only they can do that. If Matthew encounters enough rejection from the music industry, it might be the incentive he needs to make changes in his life — but that is *his* decision. (And who can say? He might just succeed!)

Young couples have their own likes and dislikes. Moreover, mothers-in-law and mothers have no more right to judge than anyone else what another should think is important. Now that you are older and more thoughtful, if you are truly honest, you know that all your children really require is your unconditional love and support. You have spent years working on these young adults, developing them into human beings — yet, now when they have matured and are married adults, you don't trust what you have accomplished. You don't give yourself credit for all those years you helped them grow. Still, somewhere in the back of your head, you must know that they are capable of thinking for themselves, that it is necessary for them to find their own place in the universe, unencumbered by *your* needs.

If you close your mind to this, you'll set yourself up for disappointment — for more hell than heaven on earth. Like Alexander Pope, it is smart to believe, "Blessed is the man who expects nothing, for he shall never be disappointed."

Most of us want to have our married children be the very best they can be, to forge another link in the family chain. If we envision a Norman Rockwell utopia for our progeny, not surprisingly, we want to live Rockwell's Thanksgiving dinner vision of the family throughout our lifetimes.

One gentleman I spoke with said, "I like the fact that my son is as giving as his mother and his grandmother — my mother-in-law — who modelled herself after her own mother." Paul told me "Always helping someone — her sense of charity really impresses me. We're Jewish, and every year at Christmas my mother-in-law bakes cookies and brings them to a Catholic orphanage, then spends the day with the children. She tells us, 'All the people of this faith are busy with their own families.'

"And even though she's in her eighties, she visits a senior citizen home, doing scutt work — sewing buttons, altering dresses, what she calls 'helping the old people.'

"And she dotes on my son. Loves us all, but Bobby is the apple of her eye. When he was young, going to Grandma's house was the best treat.

"Years ago, we were invited to a bar mitzvah. The thirteen-year-old-boys were told, 'Ask your best girl to dance,' and Bobby went straight to my mother-in-law. Today, my son is married with a child of his own, and Grandma is a shadow of her former self. But my son doesn't see that — he only sees the love she gave when he reaches out to steady her, help her across the room."

And my own children make the same kind of holiday dinners they knew growing up, serving foods I used to prepare, those favorite dishes that are expected when the family comes together at special times — thick soups and grand pies that are not altered. Recipes I used to know by heart, they have memorized. When I watch them, smiling as they strain liquids or chop onions, it enters my mind that old values are been passed on — that my children are complimenting me, saying they loved what we had.

We want for our sons and daughters-in-law to reflect us as they extend their legacy into the future, so a piece of our immortality joins the rising generation.

I asked myself, how do we mothers-in-law go about facilitating this? How do we make ourselves lovable, acceptable, maybe even cherished? I didn't have any answers. I just came up with more questions. To find a solution, an informal sampling seemed reasonable. So I asked fifty people specific questions about their mothers-in-law, about values, rituals, interests, about commonalities, what their mothers-in-law should have done that they didn't, what the interviewees would have changed, and what kind of advice they would like to pass along.

My interviews ran the gamut from young married women with infants to folks with college bound grandchildren. Some mothers-in-law spoke about when they were young daughters-in-law. They contrasted the feelings they'd had as newlyweds with those they have today as mothers-in-law and fathers-in-law.

A few responded that, if only they knew then what they know now, they would have done things differently. Others said, "I'd do everything the same!"

The individuals were of various ages, religions, and cultural and socio-economic backgrounds. Some worked; some didn't. A few were children of religiously mixed marriages, others had religiously mixed marriages of their own. In a boldly unscientific way, they were your standard Americans. Yet everyone was unique.

Different People, Different Interests

The first few questions asked were: What did you expect of your mother-in-law when you were first married? Were your expectations fulfilled? Please complete the following: "If only she would have. . . . "

Emily, a working executive in her fifties and the mother of three, said, "I expected my mother-in-law to be a second mother, someone who was fun to be with, someone I could love, someone who would love me back. But my expectations were unfulfilled. My mother-in-law was a social climber who was unhappy. She worried about how much money people had. It was difficult for me to deal with her, so I tuned out of the relationship. If only she would not have talked so much. Whatever came into her head came out of her mouth without editing."

Megan, thirty-three, is married with two children under five. "I wanted to be a good daughter-in-law. I wanted to be part of the family, and have my mother-in-law treat me like her child. We have different tastes. She's not fashionable. If she buys something it's because it's cotton, not because it's pretty. She's generous, honest, and education minded. I grew up with a negative feeling about the Catholic church, but she showed me a better side of the religion. She made me feel the church can have a positive influence in my life. If you met her you'd like her. I tend to be a pleaser, but if my mother-in-law says something, you can be sure she means it. She's outspoken. She's says things you may not want to hear, but she's often right. If only she would listen and stop talking, she'd hear a lot more of what anyone has to say. It's her biggest downfall. Another is she selectively hears what she wants to."

Elizabeth, in her fifties, a working woman with two married children, said, "I tried to get along with her. I wanted to like her, but I had faint rumblings after we met that it wasn't going to work when she told me her son was too young to marry. I was immature and she was a phony. A cold woman. A big smoocher, but there was no real warmth. She ruled the roost and wanted someone to hang on her every word. She had a genuinely good mind. It went to seed. If only she would have heard me when I tried to talk to her. Instead, she turned the conversation around and spoke about herself."

Jessica, a professional in her thirties, working, and with two children under five, said, "My mother-in-law was young and free-spirited at heart. She was a victim of the holocaust, but she never talked about it. She came to this country at sixteen, worked as a hairdresser. But she died three years after we were married. Still, she identified with young people, and it was easy to relate to her. She made me feel very included and treated me the same as my husband. If only she would not have said what she felt. Some things it's better to hold in."

Common Observations. While they were all very different, some mothers-in-law were liked more than others, but these four all had one thing in common, *none of them knew the importance of listening*. They failed to realize that when you listen to another, that person feels cared about — validated. The tendency, however, is to know better and give advice. These mothers-in-laws weren't sensitive to what their daughters-in-law needed.

Maryanne, an executive of forty with two children in college, said, "I came from a small family and thought it was wonderful to be joining a large family. I thought I'd be accepted as a daughter, but it didn't work out that way. There were generational differences. She was in her sixties, and I was married at nineteen. My parents were holocaust survivors. My in-laws were born in America but had no traditions. They let their children do what they wanted. I enjoyed being in their company because there were no rules. My mother-in-law controlled everything. Material gifts meant a lot. A label and a price tag were important. Even though she didn't have money, my mother-in-law needed the 'best,' but she never gave gifts of value back, and she never called for birthdays. She related to her daughters. If only she would have been more involved with my family."

Carole, a housewife in her fifties with two grown children, one about to be married, pointed out, "I wanted to be a good daughter-in-law to my mother-in-law. I had fun in the beginning, until I felt I was always being criticized: then I didn't like the role anymore. If only she would have accepted my husband and me for whom we were."

Jack, sixty, an executive with a married son, said, "I expected a mother-in-law who was kind and gentle, but there was no love in mine. She wanted to be better than her children, and criticized them every chance she got. This lady thrived on chaos. The only time she was kind was when someone was sick. Then she became benevolent, when she tried to be helpful. Before she died she said, 'I'm not going to leave a will. Let my children fight over whatever's left.' If only she would have been a decent human being."

Margaret, sixty, with two married children and a high-powered job, said, "I thought I'd be accepted and mothered, part of a nice Italian family, but I never experienced any warmth. My mother-in-law would speak in Italian in front of me. I don't understand the language. She was materialistic. A hoarder without a sense of humor. Everything was evaluated in money. She was totally insensitive. No matter what I did she wanted more. I learned not to trust her. Not to say anything. If only she would have shown me some affection, and not have been so angry."

Common Observations. The mothers-in-law described above were too self-involved and had insecurities that hurt the relationship. What they needed to do was look away when things bothered them, to understand that others don't live by their rules. They had to shift the focus, from themselves to their in-law child, to become a satellite instead of the hub of the universe. They ignored the fact that if you want more of something, you have to give it away. If you want more love to come into your life, the best way to get it is be more loving — more accepting. This means caring about the other's happiness as much as you do about your own.

Sam, fifty-five, a writer with two married children, told me, "I wanted my mother-in-law to stay out of my life, and she filled the bill. She was a piano teacher, bland, almost timid. I liked her. It was soothing to be with her. I felt like I didn't have to make conversation. She was not pushy like my mother, a strong lady who was like a boulder falling on a flower from a thousand feet. If only she could have. . . she would have done almost anything for us. "

Polly, a working mother in her mid-thirties with one child, beautifully described a mother-in-law close to seventy. "She's non-invasive. Not overly involved in our lives, but interested and concerned. We share the importance of family, and she says what she means. Doesn't beat around the bush. She's abrupt. It took some time getting used to. She's a very different person. I consider myself lucky because she's a very nice mother-in-law. If only she would treat her own mother nicely, but I have no idea of their history."

Daniel, a sixty-year old advertising executive with two married children, said, "I know my mother-in-law for who she is, tough as nails, but also candid with me, and I like her. I accept her with her foibles and know she's a very brave woman. She's withstood all kinds of tragedies in her life. I didn't expect anything from her — she'd already given me her daughter — but whenever you need her, she's there. That's what's important, to have people you can rely on. God help an outsider who says something bad about me — she'll rip them limb from limb. If only she had been a good girl and drunk her milk when she was young. Now she is dissolving from osteoporosis, and it's such a shame."

Elaine, a working mother in her fifties, with four children, two married, said, "I wanted to get along with my mother-in-law. She was an incredibly hard-working person, a nurse, the eldest of five, who had to raise the family. I'd known her since I was in the fourth grade. She took care of my father and grandfather when they were sick. You felt you could rely on her. She was not a complainer and always made the best of a bad situation. My mother-in-law came out of the Depression. Her father was a rancher, and she could ride a horse and shoot a gun. She instilled confidence in people. She died at age seventy-two. I grew up in the West, where people are more independent. I had a lot of freedom. I wish my mother-in-law were still around. If only she had lived longer."

Ed, president of a department store chain, a man in his late fifties with two sons, told me, "My mother-in-law was quite a bit older and strictly domestic; definitely not like my mother, who was an energetic person with a million interests and a lust for life. I didn't spend a lot of time with my mother-in-law because I wasn't looking for another important person in my life. I didn't have expectations and I didn't have disappointments.

Florence, age forty, is an executive mother with two teenage sons. "I didn't have a mother after age fourteen, so my mother-in-law became a role model for me. I admired her from the beginning. I wanted her to like me and believe I was a good wife for her son. She is a great contrast to what I knew of my mother. I'm involved with my feelings, but she can't express hers.

It's hard for me to say 'I love you' all the time, but when I do, she chokes up and says 'Me, too.' On the other hand, I hope my sons marry women without mothers. Loving to my mother- in-law means cooking or buying things. She treats me like a daughter, is generous and very straight forward. Sometimes to the point of being blunt. If only she would be her old self — she's not well physically — and be more involved in her grandsons' lives."

Common Observations. All of the above mothers-in-law got it right. They were there for their children when they were needed. They were *honest but non-intrusive,* and they understood the concept of healthy separation.

Terry, a housewife, in her fifties, has three married children. "Both of my parents were ill. I expected my mother-in-law to step in, be a mother, and to help me out, but she had an aversion to sick people. I was young and didn't understand. A nurturing mother-in-law would have suited me perfectly. If only she would have been more interested in my children. She came and sat, never did anything cultural with them. She missed out, and the kids missed out."

Kara, a housewife in her twenties, with two infants under four, observed, "I thought my mother-in-law was going to be great, and we were close, until her daughter had a child. She favors that grandchild, and that bothers me. I know when she gives me advice she's trying to be helpful, but she doesn't let up. She will suggest something and be so persistent. If only she'd babysit once in a while, and spend some more time with *my* kids."

Common Observations. One of the things children appreciate when they are in a pinch is to have family around. Mothers and mothers-in-law used to be available so that children could have a break, but society has changed. Grandmothers live far away, and of those who don't, many have jobs, or have resumed their education. Daughters-in-law may be expecting their relationship with their mothers-in-law to be the same as it was when they were kids and mothers stayed at home. They have to change that fantasy, but in the meantime, what mothers-in-law can do is go the extra mile. Put the children first. Try to balance their needs with your needs and give them the break they need.

Likes and Dislikes

The next questions asked were: What did you really like about your mother-in-law? What did you learn from her that you could pass along?

The Admired Qualities.

Simone, sixty, divorced, and a housewife with three married children, replied amiably, "I liked that she cared for me very much, and considered me her daughter. We lived next door to each other and were constantly together. She taught me how to drive and was like a mother. I learned to be supportive of my children and honest about feelings."

Linda, thirty, a housewife and mother of seven, who works part time in a school, said, "I like that my mother-in-law is open. When I was newly married she told me 'You come first. If you don't take care of yourself, no one else will. Then you won't be able to take care of your children. You'll resent them.' She has twelve children. She taught me to be strong."

Sara, fifty, a housewife and mother of three, voiced her thoughts with, "I liked that my mother-in-law gave her children an opportunity to better themselves through education. It enabled them to leave the limited circumstances of the family. She taught me that you can be independent at any age, and went to work after her husband died, having never been employed outside the home before."

Rebecca, sixty, a businesswoman and the mother of two daughters, answered, "My mother-in-law, considerably older, was a kind, gentle lady who was noninterfering, and very different from my mother who was very critical. She asked nothing of me or our relationship. She was a hard-working person with meager finances, but she found the time to keep herself looking attractive. For her generation, she was very well put together. I learned that fondest memories are left by people who cause you the least pain."

Jeff, fifty, a college professor married for the second time, commented, "I really like this mother-in-law. She's a lady! A gentle woman, well-mannered, who'd never commit a social gaff. You'd feel 'at home' in her company. She's a sensitive and intelligent person. Easy to talk to and in many respects like my mother. She also knows how to entertain. I'd like to pass along the way she has of making a person feel appreciated."

Heather, an executive in her forties and part of a religiously mixed marriage, came out with, "I like her resilience, her incredibly *up* attitude. Nothing interferes with her drive to enjoy life. I'd like to pass along her orientation to home and family life."

Valerie, forty, also in a religiously mixed marriage and a high school teacher, answered, "I really like the fact that she's there for me. Very giving of herself. She always runs over when I need a babysitter. I learned her way of trying to please people. If my mother-in-law knows you like a special dish, she brings it whenever she visits."

Andrea, a housewife in her early thirties, another person who was part of a religiously mixed marriage, stated honestly, "I like that she's generous. She'd give us the shirt off her back. What I learned from her is dedication to keeping the family together."

Cheryl, sixty, a retired counselor and the mother of two grown sons, said, "I liked the fact that she was bright and artistic and I learned kindness from her. She took our kids on trips when they were old enough to be independent."

Megan, in her thirties with children under five, commented, "I like that she doesn't forget a birthday or anniversary. She treats me as one of her family. I learned how important it is to volunteer. My mother-in-law's volunteer work reminds me of all the needy people out there, and to be thankful for what I have. To count my blessings."

Ruthanne, a widow of sixty who was part of a mixed marriage, warmly replied, "I liked that my mother-in-law was an extremely loving person. She loved me, warts and all. I was brought up as a Christian and introduced Christmas to my husband's parents. One year, my mother-in-law bought me a coat. I thanked her for the Chanukah present. She replied, 'No, it's a Christmas present.' I learned that, when you marry, you get a whole new family. That you have to adjust and be accepting of each member of it."

Daniel, in his thirties, a computer expert married for the second time, said, "I liked that my mother-in-law was graceful under pressure. She was dying of cancer when we met, but embraced life. It was a pleasure to be around her. She taught me resilience under adverse conditions."

General Observations. What each of these mothers-in-law had in common was a generosity of spirit — a genuine caring aspect. Their qualities are life enhancing. It is easy to recognize that these mothers-in-law, daughters, and sons-in-law seemed healthy and sincerely interested in each other. These children were able to see the positives and were wise enough to focus on them.

When you focus on the valuable qualities of a person, you help create a solid relationship. We place a lot of value on selflessness, but if we don't value ourselves enough we cannot give to others. These mothers-in-law had a healthy caring for themselves, so their sons and daughters-in-law were able to see them in a favorable light. It made the relationship a successful one. If you see qualities you like in another, you may incorporate these characteristics into your personality. Possibly the young women looked to their mothers-in-laws as mentors.

A wise mother-in-law can *be* a mentor, one who teaches from her experiences like a guide who shows the way. It could be as simple as how to set the table for a dinner party, carry off holiday rituals, cook for a large crowd or interview household help. It could also be more complicated — caring for an invalid child, or ailing relative. And all that you give must be in the spirit of love.

That way, it is easier for each woman to admire the other's specialness.

If you are on the side of wisdom, as these mothers-in-law were, you will look to help the younger generation. Without competitiveness, a lot of learning can take place. Treating children with respect, tolerating their foibles and acting in a loving, uncritical way, teaches acceptance. These children-in-laws were all healthy enough to see the worthy attributes of the older woman. In doing so they enriched not only their own lives but the lives of generations to come by setting a precedent of satisfying relationship skills.

The Irksome Traits

Elizabeth: "My mother-in-law was a cold woman. She always turned the conversation around and talked about herself. And she didn't listen."

Megan: "My mother-in-law hears only what she wants to. She has selective memory."

Cindy: "My mother-in-law was critical of everyone around."

Ethan: "My mother-in-law is stubborn. When she makes up her mind, proof doesn't help."

Jerry: "My mother-in-law assumes that I have the same taste as her sons."

Jessica: "My mother-in-law said whatever she felt. Sometimes it's better to hold things in.

Margaret: "When it came to gifts, my mother-in-law would say, 'Let me show you what Hannah gave me.' My gift was always compared to another's."

Judith: "My mother-in-law liked to take over. I wanted to learn how to do things, not have them done for me."

Kara: "My mother-in-law rarely visits. She doesn't spend time with my kids. It's very obvious that she's not involved with my family and favors my sister-in-law's children."

Emily: "My mother-in-law was constantly advising me. I couldn't stand it. I wish she could have accepted me for who I was."

Bill: "My mother-in-law never lets me finish a sentence."

Florence: "I'd like my mother-in-law to be more involved in her grandsons' lives."

Sara: "My mother-in-law was highly critical of all I did. She would tell me, 'You did this for your mother, but you're not doing it for me.' And she kept secrets. Talked behind people's backs."

General Observations. None of us would consider these mothers-in-law as friends. They have a "what's-in-it-for-me" attitude. They're critical and self-involved. People who are critical of others generally are struggling with self-esteem problems. Their confidence is shaky.

People often find flaws in others because if they focus on the other's imperfections, they don't have to look at themselves. Self-involvement has to do with not feeling good about who *you* are. Being critical of another implies he or she is not good enough, or can't do it, and you know better. This does not foster intimacy. Let's look at Margaret's mother-in-law. She implied that someone else's gift was more appropriate, giving Margaret the message she hadn't done it right.

These mothers-in-law seem to lack *genuineness*. In the on-going relationships, their sons and daughters-in-law experience them as mean-spirited, selfish individuals. Intruding on their children's lives, these mothers-in-law can easily become the pebble in a shoe.

What You Can Do

If you are having difficulties with an in-law situation, take a look at the following lists. Put yourself in your children's place, remember what it was like to be young, and try to recognize what they are feeling. If you can find something to identify with and say, "Yes, she might say this about me," then you can get a handle on the situation.

In ongoing family relationships you always get a second chance. However, if you remain focused on the other person's negative qualities, no change will occur because you are replaying the same old record, and are stuck in a groove of blame. What you have to do is to look at yourself and ask, "What went wrong? What can I do to make this better?" A reminder: You can't change another person, so it's up to you to respond differently.

It will be slow going, because situations don't change without effort and lifetime practices are difficult to break. Many emotions will be stirred up. To understand yourself better, it might be wise to talk about your feelings with a friend or therapist. Furthermore, keep in mind that old habits die hard, so don't give up. Work at changing because it will get you what you want — a good relationship, not only with your in-law child, but with your own child and your grandchildren. And finally, try and remember that growth is always one step beyond comfort.

Plans for the Future

Another question asked was: What do daughters-in-law have to say to the next generation of mothers-in-law?

Ten Quick Tips.

1. "Love all your in-law children. Let us know we're members of your family. Appreciate what we do for your sons or daughters, and *if you want respect, give it.*"

2. "Try to use *straight talk,* and see if you can compliment us. We know it isn't always easy. Be accepting of our flaws, and we will try to be accepting of yours, too "

3. "With holidays, please *be flexible,* and remember birthdays, too."

4. "Please listen when we talk and *hear* what we say."

5. "Visit us more often. Spend time alone with the kids. Please give them your full attention."

6. "Please *be supportive, not critical.* Recognize that kindness, and other people matter."

7. "Look to the future and not to the past. Make a life for yourself; *don't make our life yours.*"

8. *"Do things fairly* as far as gifts, so that we all get approximately the same dollar value."

9. *"Learn to back off.* Don't press us to visit more than we're able to so our meetings will be ones of joy, not obligation."

10. *"Talk directly to us.* No intermediaries, please."

Get in Touch with Yourself... then *Reach Out*

Before worrying about anyone else, you have to deal with *yourself.* Figure out your needs. Write them down. Prioritize. What is it you want from this in-law child? What is truly important to you? What can you live without?

Before sparks fly, you need to open up a dialogue with your in-law children. And it is *you* who must set aside a time to deal with the problems, when you feel comfortable about communicating your thoughts. The important thing is not to keep secrets. Secrets make people feel left out.

When an occasion arises, why not ask, "How about getting together for lunch?" Make a plan to meet somewhere neutral, and it must be a place in which you can talk comfortably. Remember, your aim is for a win-win situation, which can only take place in a relaxed atmosphere. Be considerate and ready to compromise; hear your in-law-children out, and listen for the messages beyond the words.

You need to talk, to open up a dialogue, to build trust. But be kind — realize, when you express your opinions, you are doing so to make the relationship better. And think about keeping an open mind. Hear the other's point of view. Your in-law child has a lot at stake too, and may be hurting as much as you are.

Moreover, timing is everything. If the time doesn't feel right, scrap the plan to discuss differences. Make the afternoon a social one for positive bonding, and enjoy the few hours you have together. This way you build a foundation for a future meeting.

But if everything is going well, have the strength at the right moment to speak your mind, gently. Then, take one issue at a time, in order to be sure it's resolved. If you handle too many things at once you muddy the waters, and what you wanted to resolve may get lost. And don't worry if you don't get it right the first time. Remind yourself you are capable of addressing the situation again, and be happy you took a preliminary step. Very likely, if you talk with sensitivity and only to the person involved, you will enrich your relationship with him or her.

By establishing a pattern of open communication, you lay the groundwork for solving future problems in a way that doesn't leave hurt feelings. Voice all your thoughts. Don't be afraid to say, "These were my expectations. How do they fit into yours? And if we have opposite dreams, what can we do to set our differences aside? What might we give to each other so that the two of us can live happily together?"

Family Rituals

When big cultural or religious differences hover in the background, there are usually problems to work through. You have to be more tolerant and show respect for the other person's heritage. That is harder than it sounds, because family values are loaded with judgments and strong beliefs about what is right and what is wrong, and they have been there all one's life. Even people who speak the same language have distinct philosophies, different customs, and separate ways of doing things that color feelings.

To illustrate, Betty Lee Sung, in *Chinese American Intermarriage,* says, "Mr. Woon, utterly opposed to his son's intermarriage, would repeatedly say, 'A chicken does not marry a duck.' To him, Chinese and non-Chinese were entirely different species. His arguments: The duck's habitat is the water, a chicken would drown in the pond. A duck could live on land but to deny its inherent characteristic of being an aquatic bird would go against its nature and affect its whole being."

But a Jewish gentleman who married a Greek Orthodox woman offered, "It can work, but you have to bend over backwards. In an intermarriage, everyone involved has to be willing to talk all the time, so that you are able to pick up vibrations in the air. Don't hold anything in. And you might want to consider starting off with the phrase, *'I noticed that you* . . . . Do you want to talk about it?'* Don't underestimate the value of ethnicity. It offers a new perspective to both families. Be accommodating of cultural differences and especially respectful of them at holiday time."

An American Catholic woman, married to a Spanish Catholic, pointed out that the key to a good relationship is to "focus on the similarities and ignore the trivia. Don't be too sensitive or else you give more worth to the hurtful remarks than they actually have."

And a Jewish woman married to a Catholic man said, "Respect your in-law family and treat them like they were your very own, even if you don't approve of all their ideas. You want acceptance, so learn to tread lightly. Remember that your views can change with the years."

Mothers-in-law, along with sons and daughters-in-law, have great attachments to the past, and when children marry out of their religion or culture, everyone has to learn to be optimistic and look to the future. Inevitably, there will be differences which may cause conflict and stress. In order to avoid unhappiness, and to give each person space to be a unique individual, it's best to think things out, ask yourself first: which are the most important values for you and which are least important, and identify those that cause problems.

Dealing with the December Dilemma

Differences don't disappear, so they *must* be addressed. A case in point is the "December Dilemma," the Christmas/Chanukah season, which is a big issue for many intermarried couples and their families. Instead of holiday cheer, a lot of in-laws have holiday conflict. How can this loaded issue be resolved amicably?

Talk about the December Dilemma ahead of time and introduce the meaning of your holidays, traditions, and customs to in-law children of a different faith. And if you don't understand why your in-law child has reservations about coming to a Christmas or Chanukah celebration, you might say, "What does this holiday mean to you?" Then *really listen* to the response. Ask "What is there about it that doesn't make you feel good? What did *you* do as a child growing up? What would you like from us? What ideas do *you* have that I could try? What would make *you* feel more included?" The important thing is to follow the golden rule, which is to keep an open mind.

And after the festivities are through, you might say, "I'm glad you spent Chanukah with us. Now that the holidays are over, I wonder what you're thinking. Was there anything you didn't understand? Anything that surprised you? Made you feel uncomfortable? Something you particularly liked? What can we do to make the holiday even better for you next year?"

When you fail to communicate, problems occur.

Take Christopher, for example. He comes from a strict Catholic family. His uncle is a priest; his mother goes to church every day; each Christmas, in his home of origin, there was a Christmas tree with a nativity scene underneath.

When at college, Christopher met Lori. He married her shortly after graduating. She is Jewish, and although her family follows the traditions of Judaism, they belong to a Reform congregation.

After Lori had their first child, the young couple decide to celebrate Christmas in their home. They place a Chanukah menorah in the entrance hall and a Christmas tree covered with lights in the living room, nativity scene underneath. Christopher's mother is thrilled. Christopher's mother-in-law, Daniele, a very outgoing, talkative woman, walks in, takes one look at the nativity scene, and her mouth drops. She has a hard time recovering her composure. For the rest of the day Daniele sits solemnly in a corner, feeling awful, and shortly after dinner leaves with tears in her eyes.

Had parents and children discussed the holiday before the festivities they could have avoided this situation. Nevertheless, Daniele can still talk to Christopher. She might say, "The dinner you made, Christopher, was delicious, but I'm sure you noticed I was rather withdrawn on Christmas Day. I didn't want to ruin the holiday, but I realize I must have left you confused, so I want to express my thoughts and feelings, and I would like to hear yours, too. This way we can work something out for next time."

If there is love and respect between the generations, a mutually agreeable solution will be reached, because each in-law will want to make it as comfortable as possible for the other.

...And It Doesn't End with the Holidays

Differences — individual, family, cultural, religious — are a constant dimension of in-law relationships. In the following chapter we'll take a look at some of the major issues involved when families of different cultural backgrounds or lifestyles come together.

And you thought Thanksgiving and the December holidays were a problem?

Your son and daughter-in-law have just told you that they plan to postpone children so that she can go back to school for an MBA. She has been very successful in her business career so far, and believes the advanced degree will pave the way to many more opportunities for advancement. You can barely hide your disappointment about not having grandchildren any time soon. You respond by:

    a. Letting them know you're going to change your will

    b. Telling them you don't care if they have children

    c. Crying

    d. Storming out without a word

    e. Offering to pay all their expenses for pre-natal and maternity care

    f. Asking them to tell you more about their plans and your daughter-in-law's career.

...and the result of your reaction is

    a. Anger and defensiveness on their part: "We have a right to make this decision ourselves!"

    b. Disbelief; "C'mon Mom, we know you're disappointed, but..."

    c. Guilt, and feeling sorry for you

    d. Hurt, uncertainty, frustration

    e. Refusal, anger, defensiveness: "We don't want your money; we want you to respect our decision."

    f. Openness and exchange of ideas

Chapter 4

"THY PEOPLE SHALL BE MY PEOPLE"
Marriage and Mothers-In-Law Across Cultures

*E*very culture and ethnic group has its own traditions for marriage and mothers-in-law, but the relationships vary greatly. Families everywhere have different ways of handling the union of their adult children. In contemporary America great numbers of young people — maybe most — marry partners of cultural backgrounds other than their own. (Most of us probably don't even *identify* with our own cultural backgrounds!) How does a mother-in-law — herself from a previous generation with more ties to tradition — deal with this new son or daughter-in-law who may be Greek American, Cuban American or Japanese American? Old reliable expectations may have to change, some drastically, some a little.

If you *are* a mother-in-law whose child has married a mate from a Japanese or a Greek family, you want to know something about their culture, life-long traditions, attitudes and relationships in order to bring this in-law child into the family and to avoid rejection and miscommunication. To short-circuit catastrophes before they occur, wise prospective in-laws think positively about the new family member, learn about the differences and similarities of the other, and get ready to problem solve (because disagreements will inevitably surface).

But let's start at the beginning. In America and in the middle class cultures of Western Europe, a wedding is a romantic celebration, the Cinderella story played out for real, and love marriages are the custom. Independence is promoted, and family ties are relatively weak. Young people are encouraged to find a partner who will make them *happy*. Although there are no universal prerequisites for marriage in contemporary America, most young adults believe they should be "in love" before they marry. However, it was not until the eighteenth century at the earliest that the concept of romantic marriage became common in our culture.

Arranged Marriages

The concept of marriage dates to our cave-dwelling ancestors. No doubt cavemen claimed their mates by seizing them from a neighbor, by force. Later, in an extension of the idea of "ownership," men bought wives as one would buy land, and the idea of people as property began. In early Roman law, the woman was adopted and came under the power of her husband; she literally became his slave.

When the contractual marriage came into being, a man bound his mate to him by giving a cow or other animal to the bride's family. Eventually, the husband's gift became a jewel or other article of value that went to the bride herself, and the bride received a dowry from her father when she married — a gift to her husband, whose property it became.

In more than two-thirds of the world, marriages are not always a matter of individual choice, but are based on economic exchange. Brides have a price. This way of doing things is associated with what sociologists call "patrilineal kinship," in which children of a marriage are incorporated into their father's lineage. Failure to produce a child can cancel the marriage. Parents exert a great deal of control over the young couple in these arranged marriages, largely because the marriage partners are usually too immature and the rites of the society are strictly enforced.

Family arranged marriages limit the individual's choice. If the bride and groom are consulted at all, it is only after the fact. Many times these marriages do work, of course. Good things happen, both for the adult children to be wed, and for their families.

The most famous of all daughter-in-law and mother-in-law relationships is the biblical story of Ruth and Naomi. When Naomi decides to leave the land of Moab and return to Judah, she urges her two daughters-in-law to remain in Moab. But Ruth insists upon accompanying Naomi with these words,

> *"Entreat me not to leave thee, and return from following after thee; for whither thou goest, I will go; and where thou lodgest I will lodge; thy people shall be my people, and thy God my God."*

Two strangers have grown thus to love each other.

What does anyone know of love and loving in the first years of marriage? Love grows. It takes time for any relationship to develop. How many of us fell in love at first sight?

In arranged marriages, parents may indeed form better relationships for their children because as adults they know what to look for. They can see a prospective bride or groom as the person truly is, assessing both strengths and weaknesses.

For many in arranged marriages, after twenty-five years the young couple will not have to ask, as Tevye asked Golde, "Do you love me?" Usually, they will care deeply for each other, because love can emerge in arranged marriages. It can also happen between mothers-in-law and daughters-in-law, or between any two strangers who open their hearts to each other. By doing so they become close friends.

Arranged marriages are common in Asia, Africa, parts of Southeastern Europe, the Middle East, and within certain groups in the USA, where the cultural norm is that the individual's wishes conform to the best interests of the group.

Comparing Cultural Traditions

Marriage across cultural boundaries is very common in our country. Indeed, most of us are the products of marriages which meld cultural or religious traditions, and many of us do not strongly identify with a cultural or religious background. Nevertheless, cultural and religious influences are significant factors when families attempt to join together, To explore the impact of culture on the mother-in-law relationship, this chapter examines several examples of very different patrilineal cultures.

You'll find this material of particular interest if your in-law child comes from one of these nationalities or ethnic groups, even though the marriage wasn't arranged. And, just as you may consider some of the customs of your in-laws to be unusual, they may consider yours strange also. Many groups have a xenophobic attitude toward outsiders, and might therefore express some resistance to *your* presence.

Please note that I am not a cultural anthropologist, so these comments are brief and inexact. They are based on extensive interviews with members of each group, and on research in the literature.

The descriptions that follow are necessarily general, with emphasis on the long-established traditions within each culture. Differences *within* a culture are often substantial — recent immigrants from the country of origin usually follow traditional mores closely; second-, third-, and fourth-generation American families are likely to be so thoroughly American that few traditions remain intact.

Chinese

In the United States as well as in traditional China, the family is paramount and figures principally in planning a marriage; romantic considerations rarely enter the picture. The emphasis is on obligation to the family, and children do not generally marry without the family blessing.

In their scholarly analysis, *Ethnicity & Family Therapy*, Steven P. Shon and Davis Y. Ja explain, "The individual is seen as the product of all the generations of his or her family from the beginning of time... Because of this continuity, the individual's behavior has a different importance and consequence. Personal actions reflect not only on the individual and the nuclear and extended families, but also on all of the preceding generations since the beginning of time."

Chinese sons in the USA are still as important as they were generations ago in China. They are foremost in the family, because "a son will make you a mother-in-law."

Girls in mainland China today, on the other hand, require a dowry. Depending on how strong traditional influence is on the family, this may still be the case for Chinese families in Hong Kong, Taiwan and the U.S. Because of this the Chinese say, "A daughter is a money-losing proposition," and they are brought up primarily as mates for the sons of others. Indeed, my friend Chui tells me that traditional Chinese families view a daughter as "a bucket of water — to be thrown away."

The only thing expected of a traditional Chinese bride is to please her husband and mother-in-law. "When you marry a Wu, you become a Wu. The Wus, therefore, are your first priority." By ancient custom, a Chinese bride becomes her mate's property and in effect loses her previous identity. Her job is to be faithful, not only to her husband, but to his parents.

In the past, most marriages in China were arranged by go-betweens. Today, because of the splintering of China into Hong Kong, Taiwan, and mainland China, there are many outside influences, and the traditions have been watered down. (It is worth noting that a majority of recent Chinese immigrants to the US are from Hong Kong, a very cosmopolitan city where western influences have been strong for more than a century.)

It used to be that the Chinese daughter-in-law couldn't wait for the day she herself would become a mother-in-law. That was when she became all-powerful: Her likes were considered first, her opinions counted, she was consulted before going anywhere, and her daughter-in-law had to do whatever she asked. Chinese stories are full of mothers-in law, and they are typecast along the lines of Cinderella's stepmother.

In her book, *The Joy Luck Club*, bestselling author Amy Tan tells the story of how Chinese mothers, with wounds from their terrible life in China, find themselves struggling in the United States with sons-in-law and daughters who are American, independent, and who don't understand them.

Ying-Ying St. Clair, a featured mother in Tan's novel, says, "For all these years I kept my mouth closed so selfish desires would not fall out. And because I remained quiet for so long now my daughter does not hear me. . . All these years I kept my true nature hidden, running along like a small shadow so nobody could catch me. And because I moved so secretly now my daughter does not see me. . . .

"And I want to tell her this: We are lost, she and I, unseen and not seeing, unheard and not hearing."

And when Waverly Jong brings her Anglo-American intended home to dinner, we see the chasm between the cultures. Unintentionally, the future son-in-law makes one *faux pas* after another. In one attempt to be agreeable, he endorses Mrs. Jong's disparaging remarks about her own cooking, as she politely plays down her culinary expertise. He remains oblivious to his mistake until it is pointed out later by his fiance.

My neighbor, Hoi, is from Hong Kong. "Actually, my mother-in-law's generation is hurting the most," she told me. "They bring up their children and don't get veneration. When they come to this country, the elderly are tremendously disappointed. There are big misunderstandings. Our world is so foreign. Although the mothers-in-law *are* treated with respect, the formalities are reduced, but the feelings of reverence do remain.

"Here in the United States there is a new Westernized version of the Chinese person. Be that as it may, calling a mother-in-law by her first name is unacceptable and considered insulting. The expected form is "mother," and a Chinese mother-in-law, whether in Taiwan, Hong Kong, in Communist China or in America, is still supposed to be respected.

The impact of Communism has changed many of the social mores of the Chinese people, but having a son still remains all important. Along with that goes taking care of the elderly. "You have children," another Chinese friend pointed out, "to provide for your old age."

Even though some of the old ways have been turned upside down, this friend's mother-in-law still expects her to do everything. "One day," she said, "I asked my husband to take out the garbage. My mother-in-law told me, 'I will take it out.' In a Chinese family you don't ask a husband to do *anything*. And my husband says, 'Right or wrong, you listen to my mom!' The problem is always with the daughter-in-law," my friend pointed out, "never the husband's mother."

Arranged marriages are often practiced today among Chinese here in America, where Western ideas are otherwise generally accepted. In a traditional Chinese marriage, if all the arrangements, including horoscopes (because astrological influences are important), have been worked out by the matchmaker, the bridegroom will see his bride on the wedding day. She will come to him wearing a red wedding dress. (Red symbolizes luck for the Chinese, meaning good fortune and the hope that one has a son soon. Not only is it the color of the wedding dress; the wedding seat, the candles, even the wedding gifts (usually "lucky money"), are generally enclosed in red paper or envelopes.

For wealthy people a wedding is a very elaborate and costly affair. The most important part is when the bride is carried across the threshold of her husband's home. Today this has become common practice, not only for the Chinese, but for many other Americans as well.

Your Chinese American daughter or son-in-law — if raised according to tradition — will accept you easily. They are taught to be respectful, well-behaved and, especially in the case of daughters, seen and not heard.

If you visit a traditional Chinese in-law family, leave your shoes at the door. Slippers will be provided. In the Chinese culture — as is true with American social tradition — it is polite to bring a gift when visiting; a lovely plant, flowers, or a box of candy would be appropriate.

You will find that three generations may live together in the Chinese home. The grandparents are highly respected, never slighted, and it's very important to include them in all conversations. On a first visit, don't stay too long unless invited for dinner, and refrain from being outspoken about your opinions. Instead, try hard to please. When you leave, be sure you say good-bye to the grandparents, and then invite the family to your home. (The invitation will likely be accepted, so do not offer it insincerely.)

Your new in-law family will be extremely polite and very hospitable, but don't expect a close relationship — at least any time soon. A Chinese family may feel a sense of loss if their child has chosen not to marry within the culture. It will take some time for that wound to heal. Meanwhile, you'll do best to be patient and avoid overly-friendly overtures — but don't hesitate to call now and then to say "hello," and to invite your new family to your home occasionally.

Japanese

In Japan and in the United States, most Japanese men are still looking for a girl "just like the girl that married dear old dad." Although times are changing, arranged marriages are still common. It's done quietly, usually by a matchmaker who knows each party and shows photographs to the young people. There are rigid rules to be followed. To come up with a suitable match, a resume with the complete family history, including its past and present status, along with educational and business background, is examined in detail by the matchmaker, *omiai*. The photograph, the resume, and the words of the *omiai* determine whether the young woman and man decide to meet. In 1992, thirty-two-year-old Crown Prince Naruhito of Japan reportedly considered seventy candidates who met the rigid royal requirements before he found twenty-nine- year-old, self-assured Masako Owada. Educated at Harvard and Oxford, she was a foreign ministry diplomat who understands that her marriage to the Prince now requires her to be self-effacing and to walk in the shadow of her husband.

Marriage negotiations are managed mostly by the mother, usually with the approval of her husband. When a marriage promise is made, gifts often are exchanged as a sign of acceptance of the marriage contract.

A student of mine, Michiko is on a work assignment here in the US. She was married in Kyoto in a traditional Japanese wedding ceremony. "Most Japanese weddings," says Michiko, "take place at a Shinto shrine or a Buddhist temple. The Japanese ceremony is a long one, although it usually has no religious significance, and today many brides wear white. There is much gift giving, symbols for a long and happy life together."

The Japanese mother is the primary caregiver. She spends all her time with her children, understands their personalities, and is involved in their education — in short she is totally devoted to them, and they to her. With gentle kindness, from birth she creates steel-like ties that bind her children to her, forever creating certain obligations for them. In later years the children will repeat this pattern of obedience and conformity, and carry on the same traditions with their own families.

The Japanese husband spends most of his time earning a living and has a willingness to work all kinds of hours and way into the night. Company demands seem to be the most important factor of his life. He has little time for much else.

In this culture, love and sex are not high priorities for marriage. Respect, along with companionship and raising a family, are important. Young people only go on a few dates before they have to make up their mind about a mate, because after three or four meetings, both families envision the couple getting married.

Arranged marriages are common, but no longer the rule. Before World War Two, people accepted their parents' decision regarding choice of mate without questioning. In most families, adult children born since that War have been able to refuse the parents' choice of spouse, if that person does not meet the son/daughter's expectations. But the rejection must happen right away. Michiko told me, "The whole thing is handled with much politeness. You can always say something like, 'I'm sorry, he's a good person, but we don't fit each other.' "

There is, nevertheless, a great deal of pressure to marry. Family members and friends, and even business associates can nag the young person. For a man this reaches its peak at age thirty; for a woman, generally around her mid-twenties. In fact, it is better to be a divorced woman than one who's never married, because now there is not as much shame connected to divorce. "Being single is a social curse," said *Wall Street Journal* reporter Yumiko Ono in a front-page article in the *Journal* in 1993.

In Japanese culture, as in the Chinese, the eldest son is designated to care for his mother and father, and when married, the daughter-in-law becomes part of her husband's family, and as in the Chinese culture, on the bottom rung of the ladder. Out of respect, a great sense of obligation, a desire to save "face," and attachment, the son will attend to his mother's wishes. It is especially important for the first daughter-in-law to work at achieving a good relationship with her husband's parents.

Eventually, like the Chinese daughter-in-law, she will be the one in charge. In addition, she is a role model for the other daughters-in-law.

In Japanese society, harmony is highly valued and feelings are not expressed; consequently, people must become sensitive to each other's needs. There are many subtleties in communication. The Japanese can understand each other without words, and demonstrate this through different ways of bowing, smiles and avoidance of eye contact. In America, we value verbal expression; talking too much is disliked by the Japanese. Confrontation is generally avoided.

Relationships with relatives are very important to the Japanese, and loyalty is prized. If a daughter-in-law doesn't like her mother-in-law, she still has to show up at family occasions and look as though she's happy. As she matures emotionally, she learns to be patient and diplomatic. To win approval, a daughter-in-law has to take care of her in-laws when they become old; if she doesn't and they go to a nursing home, she will be shamed. Society will ostracize her. If she does care for them, she will earn sympathy and respect, setting an example for her own children.

Your Japanese-American in-law family will welcome you and your child more quickly if you love and accept their child as one of your own. (A grandchild will facilitate the relationship, of course!)

When you are invited to visit a traditional Japanese family and meet your future in-laws, when entering their house, you may be expected to leave your shoes at the door. Like the Chinese, your hosts will provide slippers. Do not expect your Japanese in-law family to show emotion if you bring a present. They will likely not be demonstrative at all, as tradition disciplines them to keep feelings under control. The value of the gift, however, will probably be assessed — for repayment in equal value at a future time. A very expensive gift puts the recipients under an uncomfortable obligation, since custom demands that they reciprocate.

When visiting Japanese in-laws, one does not bring flowers. Flowers are generally thought of as a gift for Mother's Day or brought to people in hospitals. It is believed that white ones mean death, while colorful flowers raise the spirits and allow a sick person to heal. Food, such as fruit, cookies and candy, are good choices.

The Japanese are very sensitive to opinion. Japanese adults try hard not to offend, and they dress to fit in. Their concern is how they will be perceived. It is best to follow their lead, bow to grandparents, shake hands with the husband — but never, never hug anyone. During dinner, your food will be arranged beautifully on your plate, presented to please the eye, with as much thought given to color and texture as to taste. Let your hosts know how much you appreciate their effort. Comment on the taste of everything served. In a traditional home, you probably will use *hashi* (Japanese "chopsticks") instead of forks, knives and spoons, and might even sit on *tatami* mats instead of chairs. If so, it is bad manners for a woman to cross her legs. (Think of the picture this would make.)

Note too that the Japanese don't visit each other's homes often. Everyone keeps a respectful distance. However, relatives do usually get together twice a year, for Japanese New Year (when gifts are exchanged) and for Obon, when the spirits of dead ancestors return.

Following Japanese tradition means that you want to blend in, not stand out. When someone speaks, for example, sit up very straight, remain silent, and listen quietly. And when you leave, generously express thanks for the trouble they went to. As you exit, your hosts will generally accompany you to your car, waving energetically as you drive off, making you feel cared for, as if you were leaving for a stay abroad.

Indians

Immigrants from India residing in the U.S., bring with them a tradition of a caste system which divides millions of people into social groups. The majority of the population of India, the second most populated country in the world (China is the first) is Hindu, a religion which divides people into castes and sub-castes. It is a way of life by which families live from birth, through marriage, to life after death.

Hinduism is based on the idea that an individual's soul at death will go through a progression of rebirths. The soul's rebirth is determined by its behavior in a former life, and this is known as *karma*, the belief that no sin goes unpunished, no good deed unrewarded. Each person's actions determine whether his or her rebirth will be higher or lower. Each caste has its own complex customs as does each state, distinguished by occupation, diet, language and family practices.

In this milieu, the birth of a female child is not as welcome as that of a son, because a daughter (as in China) is considered a giveaway. In addition, when a girl marries, the father must provide her with a dowry. Usually presented to the groom's father at the engagement, this "pocket money" dowry may be used for wedding expenses, to help purchase a house, or just put in the bank. Even poor fathers feel obligated to furnish the best possible dowry for their child. If the daughter-in-law does not come with enough dowry, the mother-in-law can sometimes be very cruel, picking on her, joking about her family, and even physically harming her.

"Marriage," says my restauranteur friend Vendaya Rhasha, "is one of the most important elements of the Hindu religion, and every young girl hopes her mother-in-law will love her. For her, marriage is a religious duty that has nothing to do with romance. It is usually arranged by the heads of families to cement alliances. The preferred marriage is with a cousin."

India, like many cultures, is a patriarchal society: the father is head of the family. He often protects and controls his extended household, even after his sons are grown. He expects complete obedience from all its members, and in turn he supports them materially. It is unthinkable for anyone to question his decisions or his authority. When the father dies, the eldest son inherits his position.

The rule is submission of younger to older, and female to male. The mother is subordinate to her husband; she takes care of the home and the children. This sets the pattern for all relationships. Married sons, still under their father's influence, take their brides from their in-laws and bring them to live in their father's home.

Vendaya, who came to the U.S. just three years ago from a small town near Bombay, tells me that, "A good mother-in-law accepts the wife and makes her feel comfortable. In India, often the girls are very young when they marry and know nothing about the facts of life. This could fall to the mother-in-law, who not only has to ease her son's wife into the family, but also has to teach her daughter-in-law-about sex. Sometimes another woman in the household helps her out. Good mothers-in-law accept the new bride and try to teach her the ways of the household. Parents, and children married and unmarried, along with aunts, uncles, grandchildren, widowed sisters, and servants, often dwell in the same household."

Generally, the family instills values and privileges, and provides religious training. Being part of a joint family does not allow for much privacy, but it provides one with emotional and economic security, along with support through hard times. Children have a strong sense of belonging, each other to play with, and a close relationship with their mother, who is generally of an affectionate nature. In addition, there is bonding to several parent figures.

In India, usually, betrothals are arranged very early by parents, who look for families with similar backgrounds and beliefs. Some marriages take place when bride and groom are mere children, eight or nine years of age. This happens especially among the higher castes. At times, the child bride is so young she does not move to her husband's house until she is older (now the minimum *legal* age for marriage is sixteen for a girl and eighteen for a boy), and if the boy-husband dies, the girl is considered a widow. Widows do not remarry, and were formerly burned at their husband's funeral pyre.

Indian parents want their children to "marry up." A man may marry beneath himself, but not a woman, because her family will lose prestige in the community. If a prospective groom isn't happy with the marriage arrangement, he has the right to refuse. Today, a bride too may be consulted and often knows her intended and his family before the wedding.

"A person acceptable at one's table," says Margaret Visser, of India, in *The Rituals of Dinner*, "is also someone whose family might be eligible for alliance through marriage. Rejecting an offer of food is a sign of superiority toward the would be giver — and it inevitably means that no daughter or son of the refuser could conceivably marry a child of the refused." Consequently, it is important to know whom to invite to dinner. Issuing an invitation to the wrong person may be a social slap in the face for prospective in-laws.

Marriage is the most important ceremony in the life of a young woman. Hindus have elaborate weddings with much ceremony and feasting. The bride, who usually wears a red *sari,* receives gifts of gold jewelry and clothing that will become her property when she goes to her mother-in law's home. By marrying a man of good social standing, a woman acquires status and security — values that are very important in Indian families.

Even in America the bride is expected to be a dutiful daughter-in-law, performing all kinds of domestic work for her mother- in-law, who runs the house. It is the daughter-in-law who has to do the adjusting, and be the one to change. In the beginning she may be treated like an unpaid servant. She was taught as a young child to be tolerant, humble, caring with older people. She learned to be respectful of others, and to bend over backwards and give in, because getting along will be a major part of her life. Moreover, most of her life is devoted to family. She rarely sees her own parents, usually only at festival times. And her parents don't want to see her: If she comes home too often, people may think something is wrong with the marriage.

A daughter-in-law gains importance when she becomes a mother because mother is the symbol of love. Most of these arranged marriages work out, owing to similarities of caste, religion, and economic background, and these ties that keep the young couple together eventually foster love.

If you visit a Hindu Indian family, you will, in this culture too, take your shoes off at the door. At dinner, eating only with your right hand, you will try foods seasoned with many spices. Your Indian hosts may use their fingers to bring food to their mouths. Don't expect to be served beef. Cows are sacred animals to Indians. Generally, alcoholic beverages are not consumed.

The New Year holiday — "Diwali" — is important in India. In Bombay at this time, the fronts of houses are decorated with lights and designs of colored powder. Friends visit each other and lots of food is served.

As is true in many cultures with long traditions, it is important to be respectful to the older generation. When elders enter a room, for example, you get up to receive them and then sit only when they sit. An Indian mother-in-law will never have her legs exposed, for it is the custom when not wearing a *sari* to wear pants. Indian women are charming, compliant, colorful, and bend over backwards to be kind.

If your child marries a Hindu Indian, you will want to respect social tradition and telephone the in-law parents once in a while. Be open-minded and treat your new daughter/son-in-law as if she/he were your own flesh and blood.

Greeks

In Greece, a country that has produced some of the most brilliant minds civilization has known in its philosophers, dramatists, mathematicians, and historians, generally a male-oriented society exists today. Even here in the United States family authority rests with a strong father who is convinced that a woman's place is in the home.

Girls are not considered as important as boys, since their marriage takes them to their husband's family. In Greece, as well as in America, mothers-in-law, mothers, and children are treated as subordinate figures with limited liberty — but a mother's kindness and hospitality are known far and wide. (Stephanos Zotos explains in *The Greeks: The Dilemma of Past and Present*, that, during the German occupation of Greece, many Greeks hid Jews in their homes. "When asked about why they had risked their lives, most of them answered that hospitality in Greece was sacred and that what they did was nothing extraordinary.")

Generally, a Greek woman doesn't disagree with her husband publicly or raise her voice. Her job is to take care of the home and family, and her home is a warm, child-centered affair. However, many women today, in Greece and in the United States, work in their husband's businesses.

In the United States a Greek mother is close to her children and made to feel responsible for the way they turn out. "There is no back talk in a Greek home; you do not oppose your elders." My guide here is Nick Kostopolous, a teacher at the high school near my home. "There are many quarrels between relatives, and much competitiveness. One part of the family is always jealous of the other."

The ancient quest for knowledge is still very much alive, because *achievement* is the operative word in the family. Children, here, where the Greeks have assimilated, still retain old values. "They are expected to work hard in school, and make their parents proud," Nick tells me. "When their youngsters are grown and married, mothers-in-law prefer to live in close to them. Greek women have strong family ties and traditions."

In Greece and here in America, marriage is the focus of a girl's life, and women are expected to marry before the age of thirty.

Children are taught that security is more important than love so when marriages are arranged, mates are chosen for status and financial gain. The father chooses the bridegroom, and the bride goes from the parental home to the bridegroom's home. Psychotherapist Eva Primpas Welts points out, in her "Greek Families," a chapter in *Ethnicity and Family Therapy,* "Many young women achieve the illusion of free choice and avoid open confrontation with their families by seeing to it that they only fall in love with men who will please their parents.

"Women who have passive husbands usually maintain them as figureheads, while they establish their own rules. There is a folk saying that acknowledges the influence of women: 'The husband is the head, but the wife is the neck which decides which way the head will turn.' " In many households, it's the woman who manages the money and doles it out as she sees fit.

Greek men are devoted to their mothers who receive a great deal of affection from them. This can annoy wives who wind up having to take a back seat to their mothers-in-law. Yet in old age it is the daughter who usually cares for her parents, and the son who, after his father's death, heads the family.

If your child marries a Greek American, it's almost certain that you will find him or her — and the in-law family — warm and affectionate. These are people who like to embrace each other. They hug and kiss on both cheeks. This is a friendly expression, not a romantic-sexual one. And your in-law family will want you to respond in kind, not be stand-offish. Family is very important to the Greeks. At holiday time they want to be with their children, and their children's families — that means you, the in-laws. They never want to be left out of parties or events, and their hospitality is unmatched.

When you visit this in-law family, bring cookies or flowers. Gifts are important; Greeks are big gift-givers. When a girl becomes engaged, mother, mother-in-law-to-be, aunts and cousins usually give her pieces of jewelry: bracelets, gold coins, necklaces, even family heirlooms.

Don't be afraid to taste the food they offer, the wonderful eggplant dishes and honeyed sweet cakes. Try everything, even if it's just a tiny bite. They'll appreciate it. And do speak up. Greeks are not shy; they like to talk. Compliment them, say lots of nice things, but stay away from both political and monetary subjects. You should then have a cordial, even warm relationship with your new friends, your in-law children's parents.

Lubavitcher Hasidim

In the United States, the Lubavitcher sect of Hasidic Jews is a small subgroup of the population of American Jewry that emigrated from Eastern Europe. Boys and girls don't mix. The children attend separate schools, and the boys spend most of their time in religious study, from early in the morning to after nine in the evening.

The girls study, too, though they have a shorter day and rarely go to college. The young woman's major concern is, will she have a family? Her goal is the same as that of her mother and mother-in-law to be; that is, to get married, have children, and educate them in their Jewish heritage and traditions. Learning permeates every element of Hasidic family life, and children acquire status by how learned they are, not by whom they date.

When young adults meet, it is a serious meeting for the purpose of marriage, and to have the option of choosing someone suitable. The average age of marriage is between eighteen and twenty-three for a Hasidic woman, between twenty and twenty-five for a man.

A sensitive matchmaker, called a *shadken*, is contacted, and this person investigates the families and the prospective bride and groom. A lot of research goes into the marriage arrangement. It is not a hit-and-miss affair but a serious undertaking, and the goal is a merger of families. Both sets of parents get a verbal resume before anything takes place. The matchmaker may be a cousin or aunt who will speak with both parties. He or she fills in all the unknown details and quietly arranges when and how the date will take place. The presence of a third party reduces the stress level and the awkwardness of the situation. After the date is over, the matchmaker meets with the respective families to discuss whether the two people are compatible.

I said to one Hasidic woman who had been married for twelve years, "You hardly knew your husband. What made you think the marriage would last?" She replied, "You have to have faith that God will take care of you."

"Children's duties to parents are rooted in religious principles, not the least of which is the commandment to honor one's mother and father," say Fredda M. Herz and Elliot J. Rosen in *Ethnicity and Family Therapy*. "This concept of *mitzvah*, or obligation, is central in Jewish tradition and results in a plethora of 'shoulds' and 'musts' that are an aspect of the family ethos."

The Lubavitcher are a very close-knit group. Mother is in control. She rules the house, sets the tone, is the communicator and the nurturant member of the family — the one who feeds the children (there may be ten or more in a typical family), teaches them, tends them when sick, babysits the infants, supplies affection, and settles disputes.

Among Hasidim, ties to the family remain close even after a marriage occurs. A son comes to his in-laws when a baby is born, and usually for holidays — and there are many holidays in the Jewish religion. The son-in-law or daughter-in-law may move into the in-laws' home for days or weeks at a time. The mother-in-law is not fazed by this — she is used to having a lot of people around.

One of the reasons the mother-in-law is held in high esteem in Hasidic tradition is that she is not only resourceful and learned, but is typically so busy with her own brood she doesn't have time to mix into her married children's affairs. While her adult children are raising their youngsters, she may still be coping with five or six little ones of her own. Her focus is upon her immediate family life and not on living vicariously through her married children. She lives to see *nachas* (joy) — a form of achievement from her offspring.

Another thing that may factor into the closeness between daughters-in-law and mothers-in-law in the Hasidic community is that there is very little generation gap. Older Hasidim receive enormous respect; they are revered by their children. The Hasidic woman I spoke with said, "My mother-in-law sees the hand of God in everything. She taught me to, 'Be the best I can be,' and that is something I'd like to pass along to my own children."

Hasidic mothers-in-law and mothers are the only role models for daughters and daughters-in-law. The aim for mothers-in-law is the same as for mothers: to have children and educate them.

Should you become a mother-in-law to a member of this religious group, you will want to know a few of the Hasidic customs. Women and men do *not* shake hands. When visiting Hasidic in-laws, a mother-in-law would be smart to wear a long-sleeved, high-necked dress. A gift of flowers would be very acceptable but stay away from foodstuffs or drinks. As for conversation, a "live-and-let-live" attitude serves best. Refrain from bringing up any controversial subjects; safest grounds are recipes, children, and the home and furnishings.

Guatemalans

Guatemala has the world's largest population of pure Indians, more than fifty percent. They are direct descendants of the Mayans, and most still preserve the primitive customs and traditions their ancestors knew centuries ago, although their small country is heavily influenced by its (usually wealthier) citizens of European descent.

The native Mayan-Indians speak more than twenty languages with over one hundred dialects, and the women, even today, grind corn by hand. The women of San Pedro, on the shores of Lake Atitlan in the southwestern highlands, marry men of their own villages, carry babies on their arms, are creative weavers, laugh and joke easily in their own domain, are authoritarian with their children, and keep their faces half-hidden in a shawl they wear in public. During the day they cannot speak to a man who isn't related to them without arousing suspicion.

As is true in many cultures, a double standard exists. Boys, from the age of twelve, are taught about sexuality from older youths, and the practice of sex is accepted by men. Women who enjoy sex, however, are considered witches. One consequence is that it is considered immoral for a wife to assume any but a passive position in sex. Although adultery is supposedly sinful for both sexes, men are expected to take advantage of whatever comes their way. A widow who tills her own corn fields borrows a child from a neighbor to accompany her so she will not be approached sexually.

Women are expected to be submissive, with little display of emotion. This is role-modeled for female children, who are extremely docile and modest. They are taught early to keep their skirts below their knees and shawls over their heads. There is no sex education for them. Even if mothers wish to break with the past, to tell their daughters about sex, they are inhibited by their own superstitious upbringing.

Menstruation, for example, is a mystery that comes as a shock to a young girl. She is taught to keep her bleeding a secret and that after marriage she must avoid intercourse during her periods. Lois Paul in "The Mastery Of Work And The Mystery Of Sex In a Guatemalan Village" in *Woman, Culture, and Society* explains: "An old woman complains: 'It is very bad for a man to have intercourse with his wife when she has her "flower" (period), because a long thing like a rope inside the woman descends and beats him when he enters her.' "

In Guatemala, courtship generally takes place when a girl is thirteen or fourteen years old. This is the only time she exerts power over a male. The young woman tends to prolong this period, because by seventeen (it can be even fifteen), she is already a bride, and the man, as tradition dictates, has had his parents ask for her hand. Outside of a few words spoken, the couple do not know each other or how to communicate, and the new wife has little knowledge about the mechanics of sex — she has never been without clothing, even when bathing. A bride, a virtual stranger who now lives with her husband's family, may spend a terrifying wedding night shrieking in bed. Sometimes, the mother-in-law has to calm the young woman. Once more Lois Paul clarifies: "The culture of San Pedro assigns pleasure to the male and reproduction to the female."

Giving birth raises the standing of the bride in her husband's household. It is a most important transition, for it provides proof of fertility and rekindles ties with her own family. It is the mother-in-law who judges that the daughter-in-law is pregnant. (Pregnancy too, is clothed in mystery.) "The Guatemalan mother-in-law controls and conducts the pregnancy," observes Sheila Kitzinger in *Women As Mothers*, "and the expectant mother herself is not even supposed to know she is pregnant. The mother-in-law arranges for the midwife to call regularly, to 'cure her sickness' and make her periods return, and this fiction is maintained by all. Moreover, if the pregnant woman does not obey her mother-in-law and fulfill her obligation as a good wife and daughter, she puts the fetus in peril, and the baby may die."

The mother-in-law increases her watchfulness until the young woman gives birth. It is her function to be a mentor, to instruct in family tradition, and to hand down local lore. More than that typically happens during the pregnancy; a closeness develops, trust grows into love and the two women bond. Kitzinger goes on to point out that a mother-in-law's function is significant in terms of continuity. "She acts as the ritual agent between past, present and future." Through the painful rite of pregnancy, a bride wins the day and becomes a woman. For the first time she is aware of sexual knowledge that only experienced females have and she can use it as a source of power — even a weapon — to control her husband. A wife feels a connection with all the other women with the birth of her first child; she learns that a woman's body has magical (life-giving) powers. But conforming to the behavior of the group, she remains silent about sex and reproduction, thereby perpetuating the mores of that culture.

In the United States, Guatemalans as a rule are working-class people who have strong family ties, and live in close proximity to one another. Large populations live in Southwestern urban centers, especially in Los Angeles and Houston. A fair number live in New York, particularly in the Flatbush section of Brooklyn. Guatemalans, like most immigrants have preserved their traditional views in this country. Roles are defined; the husband dominates and is the provider for the family. The mother, although devoted to home and children, also works. The live-in mother-in-law does the chores, cooking, and cleaning. She nurtures the children, who are very close to their grandparents.

If your child marries a Guatemalan, and you are invited to meet your future in-laws, come with a smile and a cake. Be friendly but respectful. Respect is highly valued in this culture, and listening carefully when someone speaks is part of that respect. You'd be wise not to interrupt, even if you disagree. Though rarely a trusting people, Guatemalans are nevertheless hospitable. They will prepare a dinner for you that includes tortillas and rice. The parents I spoke with were warm, honest, and concerned about the welfare of their children. One said, "When they marry, they should find someone who knows what they are worth."

Cubans

Cuba, the largest island in the Caribbean and once an important commercial and political center, was a place where the men provided the money, and the women, devoted to their children, stayed home. Many had servants, and Mother, who took pride in dressing up, was considered the lady of the house.

After the communist revolution of the 1950s, many Cubans left their country, emigrated to the United States and settled in metropolitan areas in Florida, New York, New Jersey, California and Illinois.

In these Cuban enclave communities, where the religion is Catholic, a re-Cubanization has taken place. Another world exists here — you can almost feel the tropical atmosphere, and the rhythms of Latin music are heard in the streets. Ethnic traditions are affirmed, and the language in the air is Spanish. Children, although bilingual, still learn this language as their mother tongue.

Cuban Americans, the third largest Hispanic group in the United States, are a successful minority of survivors in which, in most cases, the male still reigns supreme.

The first group of Cubans to leave their island were white, upper- and middle-class professional families who came to the United States sometime between 1959 and 1965. Carmen is a first-generation Cuban-American. "When I arrived here in 1962," she told me, " I wasn't allowed to bring anything with me except the clothes I wore. When I visited the Holocaust Museum in Washington DC many years later, I cried like a baby because I could sympathize with the Jews. I, too, had to start a new life in this country, and I can never go back. I left my country looking for freedom and I found it here."

The second wave of immigrants, too, were mostly middle class: small businessmen and skilled laborers, and again predominantly white. The third, largest, and youngest group of Cuban immigrants — the "Mariel boat people" — arrived after 1980.

"The people arriving here in the 1990s," Carmen explained, "are coming supposedly for political reasons, but they are really suffocating economically in Cuba. Today, you can't buy anything in Cuba without U.S. dollars. Relatives are writing for money; it's a matter of survival."

Many Cubans had problems with gender-role reversal after their arrival: men were unable to find jobs and the women went to work. This caused changes in family interactions, giving the wife more equality in decision making, especially if she had better social skills. Difficulties arose when wives wanted help with child care. Cuban men resisted. When they did help, it was because they chose to do so. The Cuban woman who has power is careful to play it down; she may even give up her independence so as not to threaten her husband's dominance.

One Cuban woman admitted, "Women are strong, but men are head of the house. Women play the game in front of people. A wife will let her husband be the master. She knows how to manipulate him to get what she wants."

When asked how she does that, I heard, "Crying. Tears. Cooking what he likes."

Cuban Americans remain a formal and polite people, a people with a great sense of family loyalty, where parents take care of grandparents and three generations not only live together but interact a lot. In this atmosphere the mother-in-law is most helpful. She expects obedience and wants to know what's going on in the lives of her children — every minute. In return, she will always, always be there for them. Children of this culture depend on their parents, who are gracious and very giving but raise their youngsters strictly. Grandchildren are loved and spoiled and learn early that whatever the teacher says is law.

Good Friday and the Holy Week are very important to Cubans. Thanksgiving is considered an unimportant Anglo holiday, but Cubans celebrate it anyway, with rice and beans and turkey

"Cuban style." At Christmas, they celebrate the Eve, not the Day, and give presents to children on January 6.

An Anglo woman married to a Cuban told me, "A Cuban mother-in-law will do *anything* for you. Cook. Take care of the kids. Do laundry. What she wants in return is respect, and once in a while to be taken out to a restaurant. They are warm and helpful, but they don't say what they want right out. Normally, there is a lot of beating around the bush."

Cuban exiles who have lived in the United States many years often have a more egalitarian outlook, especially if they have moved away from Cuban communities. Although they lead a life similar to that of most other American families, they approach things differently. If possible, the women want to stay home. Most are devoted to their children and do not want them to live on their own. When children get married they move out. Even when they are grown, children are encouraged to live close to their families — there is much camaraderie, and they call Mother "Mami," a very warm version of "Mom."

Cubans worry about what "outsiders" think. The family, including cousins, aunts, uncles, nieces, nephews, friends, and neighbors are very important, and you do things to make your family look "good." Many Cuban children, like most immigrants before them, bring pressure on their parents to change — to "Americanize" — in hopes that they will be better accepted by their schoolmates.

Cuban women are expected to be faultless housekeepers. A clean house is a big asset, and every mother-in-law wants her daughter-in-law to have a spotless home, and to be devoted to the grandchildren. Grandmothers spoil their grandchildren. They take pride in sewing and knitting for them, dressing them in homemade clothes. Cubans like everyone to be properly dressed, especially for social occasions. When they party — and Cubans do enjoy partying — they like to "dress to kill."

In this culture it is not uncommon for a certain amount of rivalry to exist between mothers-in-law and mothers. On Mother's Day, I was told, "It's wise to buy the same gift for both."

On Sunday afternoon, you are expected to visit either your mother or mother-in-law for the traditional meal. At two o'clock, *almuerzo* is served, a complete meal, with the whole family sitting around a huge table. One week you go to your mother's house, the next week to your mother-in-law's.

A Cuban woman mentioned, "There are a lot of strings on married couples. The husband's mother is always watching her daughter-in-law, and they don't believe in babysitters. In-laws and parents give a lot of support, but everyone also gives a lot of advice, too.

"There is pressure on the children to conform. A mother-in-law, the mother of the son, rules the nest. She helps a lot but feels she can tell her grown children what to do. Also, having a son is very important. It's through the son that the name in most cultures is passed on."

Many Anglo Americans marry Cubans, and if your child is one of them and your in-laws invite you to visit, you must *never* refuse food. It is impolite. What Cubans like to hear is, *"This is delicious,"* even if you can't swallow it. Do come dressed up, and bring wine or something homemade — cookies or cakes — as a gift. And make an effort to speak Spanish. Even if you just attempt to say a word or two, it will show the parents of your son or daughter-in-law that you care about their culture. Cubans are extremely generous, loving, caring, amiable, warm and huggy, and open-hearted. They are a generous people who will offer the shirts off their backs — though nobody ever handed them anything.

Bridging the Culture Gap

Intercultural marriages are commonplace in the U.S., yet it's rare to experience a marriage of "pure" cultural differences. Most of us have something of a "distant-but-warm" identification with a particular culture, since we are likely to be a blend of several backgrounds. The discussions of cultural concepts of marriage and family in this chapter have focused on relatively clear-cut traditions — traditions that are probably practiced here only by first-generation immigrants.

Nevertheless, it is worth noting the several themes that emerge from this informal survey. Mothers-in-law and prospective mothers-in-law whose children have selected partners from other backgrounds may well wish to consider the following suggestions common to nearly all the cultures described:

• Recognize that it is still a male-dominated world, and that brides, mothers and mothers-in-law continue to fight an uphill battle for respect and recognition in the family in most cultures.

• Learn as much as you can about the culture that will become a part of your family quilt.

• Patience and tolerance are the most important single strengths required to bridge culture gaps. It takes time to learn about each other, and to accept our differences.

• Try to visit with your new in-laws often, within the traditions of the new culture, so you can get to know both them and their culture.

• Beware of generalizations about a culture — even those presented in this chapter. Families vary greatly in their commitment to cultural traditions.

• Focus your attention and your affection on your daughter- or son-in-law.

• Be yourself; don't pretend to be a member of your in-laws' culture.

• Don't try to buy the affections of your in-laws. You don't want to embarrass them, or create uncomfortable obligations, with inappropriately expensive gifts.

• Don't expect your in-law family to be as social as the neighbors on a TV sit-com. They may require a good deal more privacy.

• Allow your son- or daughter-in-law to guide you in relating to his or her family and its culture, but do your own bridge-building.

Two Sides of the Coin

When it comes to marriage in most societies of the world, and even in certain groups here, the obligation to one's parents supersedes self-gratification. In-laws in some ethnic groups have enormous power. Generally, they use it wisely, because most have their child's interest at heart. Many arranged marriages — perhaps most — are successful largely because of common bonds of culture, education, religion, and economics.

Maybe being in love just isn't enough. The expectation for those who believe in the Cinderella myth is that everything will remain the same, that intense passion produced by youthful hormones will sustain through the years, and that bride and groom will experience an emotional high forever. Those of us in long-term marriages know that this is impossible, and such naivete a set-up for emotional disaster.

A lasting love encompasses compatibility, trust, commitment, respect, companionship, objectivity, compassion, tenderness, forgiveness, and an understanding of the human frailties — along with meeting the romantic and sexual needs of the partners. Whether in arranged marriages or love marriages, the expectations of parents, in-laws, and bride and groom are that the union will result in the fulfillment of these goals, that the young couple will truly love each other. In fact, as Erich Fromm points out in his classic treatise, *The Art Of Loving*, "To love somebody is not just a strong feeling — it is a decision, it is a judgement, it is a promise. If love were only a feeling, there would be no basis for the promise to love each other forever. A feeling comes and it may go. How can I judge that it will stay forever, when my act does not involve judgement and decision?"

Those who are married have to travel similar paths. The goals for all people in a relationship are the same. The hope is that the love you seek will occur, and that you will become connected, not only to your mate, but to family members, friends, and in-laws, so that eventually you may be able to say the words "I love you" to all of them — and mean it.

Sources (Please see additional sources in the Bibliography, page 217.)

Chinese

Porter, Katherine Ann. *Mae Franking's My Chinese Marriage.* Austin: University of Texas Press, 1991.

Shon, Steven P., and Davis, Ja Y. "Asian Families" in *Ethnicity and Family Therapy*, Edited by Monica McGoldrick, John K. Pearce, and Joseph Giordano. New York: The Guilford Press, 1982.

Sung, Betty Lee. *Chinese American Intermarriage.* New York: Center for Migration Studies, 1990.

Tan, Amy. *The Joy Luck Club.* New York: G.P. Putnam's Sons, 1989.

Cubans

Bernal, Guillermo. "Cuban Families" in *Ethnicity and Family Therapy*, Edited by Monica McGoldrick, John K. Pearce, and Joseph Giordano. New York: The Guilford Press, 1982.

Gann, L.H., and Duignan, Peter J. *The Hispanics In The United States: A History.* Boulder: Westview Press, 1986.

Richmond, Marie LaLiberte. *Immigrant Adaptation and Family Structure Among Cubans in Miami, Florida.* New York: Arno Press, 1980.

Greeks

Welts, Eva Primpas. "Greek Families" in *Ethnicity and Family Therapy*. Edited by Monica McGoldrick, John K. Pearce, and Joseph Giordano. New York: The Guilford Press, 1982.

Zotos, Stephanos. *The Greeks: The Dilemma of Past and Present.* New York: Funk and Wagnalls, 1969.

Guatemalans

Kitzinger, Sheila. *Women As Mothers.* New York: Random House, 1978.

Paul, Lois. "The Mastery of Work and the Mystery of Sex in a Guatemalan Village" in *Women, Culture and Society.* Edited by Michelle Zimbalist Rosaldo and Louise Lamphere. Stanford: Stanford University Press, 1974.

Indians

Stacy, Allen. *Visiting India.* New York: Hippocrene Books, 1986.

Visser, Margaret. *The Rituals of Dinner.* New York: Grove Weidenfeld, 1991.

Wilber, Donald N. *Pakistan.* New Haven: Hraf Press, 1964.

Collier's Encyclopedia 42 ed., s.v. "Hinduism."

Collier's Encyclopedia 42 ed., s.v. "India."

Collier's Encyclopedia 42 ed., s.v. "Marriage."

Japanese

Bumiller, Elisabeth. *The Secrets of Mariko: A Year in the Life of a Japanese Woman and Her Family.* New York: Random House, 1995

Hamabata, Matthews Masayuki. *Crested Kimono.* New York: Cornell University Press, 1990.

Kahn, Herman. *The Emerging Japanese Superstate Challenge and Response.* Englewood Cliffs, New Jersey: Prentice-Hall Inc., 1970.

Ono, Yumiko. "Irked Brides in Japan Practice a New Rite: Ditching the Groom." *Wall Street Journal,* January 4, 1993.

Lubavitcher Jews

Rabbi Naftali Brawer.
Herz, Fredda M., and Rosen, Elliot. "Jewish Families" in *Ethnicity and Family Therapy,* edited by Monica McGoldrick, John K. Pearce, and Joseph Giordano. New York: The Guilford Press, 1982.

You're getting together with your new daughter-in-law's parents for the first time. Naturally you want everything to go well, so you're trying to decide what to tell them about your family. You believe it's important to be honest and open, so you elect to say:

　　a. "I think Senator Blowhard will make a great president, don't you?"

　　b. "Some of my best friends are (Chinese, Jewish, Mormon...)"

　　c. "We never watch television!"

　　d. "The problem with this country is too many of them."

　　e. "Has Fred told you our famous family story about his Uncle Harold?"

What happens next?

　　a. Are you sure you want to discuss politics the first time you meet the family?

　　b. If your goal is to let people know you accept them, this isn't the way.

　　c. Your snobbery is aimed at about 97% of the population.

　　d. Whoever they are, such intolerance is likely to cause trouble.

　　e. If the Harold story is funny and tells something informative about your family, why not? Just give some thought to (1) will they be interested? (2) does the story not ridicule anybody (e.g., religion, culture)? (3) will it help conversation along, or cut it off?

Chapter 5

NOT-QUITE IN-LAWS
When Your Child Is Not Married

*W*hen I grew up, I was committed to finding a mate I could live with the rest of my life. When he came along I thought, "This is a person to build a family with." I bought the whole package — for better or worse, richer or poorer — and made a lifetime commitment. The expectation was not to have a Mercedes in the driveway, but to make the marriage work.

Commitment is a living thing, requiring an understanding of someone else's needs without giving up one's own identity, adapting and growing to changes the years bring. Many evenings my husband and I had to acknowledge we had problems to work through. And we did, because we focused on commitment. It was there always.

Each stage of life has its own commitments, of course. The birth of our children brought us new ones. And as the children grew, we tried to mold them, hoping to introduce the right ingredients into their young minds.

In my mind's eye I saw them as people who would learn to form strong bonds, as men and women able to value themselves, our family, and their own future families. I wanted them to reap the benefits of our commitment and eventually to make commitments of their own.

A lot of people have concerns about committing to something they have to stick with. Nowadays everyone seems to want options. Alas, marriage doesn't come with a guarantee, and a million divorces a year is a lot. In-laws and parents alike may whisper, as each child walks down the aisle, "I hope this one will last."

Most parents have visions of their children's weddings, picturing a daughter in a haze of tulle, a son in full dress. But it doesn't always work out that way. Lots of young adults these days elect to live together without getting married, or they choose other non-traditional lifestyles. Many of these young people say, "Fifty percent of those who marry end up in divorce." Many parents worry about the way children are staying single, while the children worry about making a commitment.

(The "fifty-percent" statistic is wrong, incidentally. The actual fact is that nationwide there are about half as many divorces as marriages — one million divorces, two million marriages — in any year. Some demographers — and hordes of journalists looking for a headline — call that a "50% divorce rate." But the one-million divorces occur among 30 million married couples; an actual rate of just over three percent!)

Whatever the exact numbers, there can be no argument that millions of families have adult children who are not in traditional marriages. To better understand the role of these parents — the "not-quite in-laws" — I sought out and interviewed, in an unscientific way, dozens of people who had children in long-term relationships. My goal was to present a wide variety of connections — to show how men and women nowadays are redefining family patterns.

I talked with mothers, fathers, mothers-in-law and fathers-in-law. The families included both parents and adult children who are in traditional marriages, divorced-on-speaking-terms, and divorced with no communication. I interviewed adult children who are still single by choice, and a number who live homosexual lifestyles — with and without long-term partners.

So that this chapter might help parents better understand the adult children's needs — and their own, my interviews explored such topics as disappointments, losses, gains, feelings, the future, and what it's like being a not-quite in-law.

Parent Perspectives on "Living Together"

I asked parents of children in long-term relationships: *Has your child's lifestyle affected your life? What do you say to yourself? How do you let your child know you love him/her? What advice can you offer to parents who have a similar situation?* Here is some of what I learned:

• Claudine said, "I have a grandson and I don't have a grandson, because my son never married and he's no longer with the mother of his child. This has left me without a daughter-in-law to talk to, and deprived me of seeing my grandson grow up. I feel sad that I can't have a relationship with my not-quite in-law. But my son warned me to be wary, and being on guard makes me feel uncomfortable, so to protect myself I stay away. When I speak to my son, it's hard getting him to talk about my grandson.

"He tells me Jonathan can write his name, but not the cute things he does, and there is lots that I'm missing. This situation has made me leery about my son's other relationships. He's dating. There's been a succession of girls, but I don't want to get involved.

"How do I deal with my feelings? I talk to close friends, and this helps. And I eat — that's what I do that's negative, and then I tell myself my son has many good traits and make room for my other grandchildren.

"I'd advise other parents not to question your child about his/her partners, and don't withdraw your affection. Trust your child to work out his/her life without you. Maybe love is not criticism."

Our culture has created new societal configurations. Claudine is a grandmother who has a tenuous connection with her grandchild and her not-quite daughter-in-law. The blood connection makes the relationship with the child important, but is it possible? One optimistic solution might be for Claudine to reach out to her son's ex, to try to build a bridge that would allow them to work together, and to hope that the young woman would be open to a relationship. Such a move is risky, and she'll need to start cautiously — a step at a time.

• Tricia told me, "I'm happy that my son is happy and has someone in his life, and I feel better that he has *one* special person rather than playing the field. I'm very fond of the woman he's with, and think of her as my future daughter-in-law.

"They've been together two years, and we have a particularly close relationship. If they break up, I'll feel very sad, as if a marriage broke up, but I'm hoping it's going to grow into something more formal — marriage.

"This relationship has been very good for my son. Both he and his girlfriend know their present arrangement is okay with me, because I, too, am living with a man. It's also not a marriage, but it is. This is what middle America is all about.

"My advice to parents is, when young people are happy and love each other, give them your blessings!"

This son is following his mother's pattern. Tricia and her family seem to be taking part in a new cultural norm, which declares, "This is what people do today."

• Arthur said, "My child has left me in an in-between state. I never know if the woman he lives with is a member of my family or not. I feel she is, but I can't acknowledge her that way. I work within his framework, but it's not satisfying. My child is very conservative in most ways. This is the only area in which he is not a traditionalist."

"What do I do with my feelings? Not much. I want my child to be happy, and as long as he is, I accept my limitations in changing the situation."

• Michael told me, "I think my daughter is going to get hurt. To me, she's like a child playing house. I think our lives should be based on what's legal, and 'living together' is half a commitment — a waste of time. If you feel the relationship is right, then you get married. Living together is the end of a generation; that part of the family dies.

"But, on the other hand, if it's good enough for my daughter, it has to be good enough for me. I love her and she knows it, and I'm supportive. I'd like my daughter to have stability, marriage, a family. To have her know the goodness there is in watching a child grow — see dreams materialize. Without children, you'll never have that joy. I don't think it's possible with just a 'relationship.'

"The advice I'd give? Accept the situation as quickly as you can. You might try to influence your children, but you have to know when to keep quiet, too. Most of the time they don't hear what you say, so learn to cry in silence."

Arthur and Michael are struggling, trying to come to terms with the relationships their children have established. They feel the strain of not-quite having an in-law child. The love of the fathers for their children comes through in both cases, as does their strong traditional values. It seems that both men are trying to move beyond the old family patterns, to make new boundaries for themselves.

• Julie said, "My son's relationship hasn't affected me, except that I want to win the young woman over, because I'm afraid if I don't, I'll lose my child.

"I've been through this before, and I get involved in his relationships; then, when they end, I have no mourning period, and it's like falling off a cliff.

"I never go shopping without thinking, 'Wouldn't this look cute on his latest girlfriend?' At the same time, I tell myself, If I was intelligent, I'd stay away, but I don't want to lose my son, so basically I accommodate myself to his needs, and I feel I'm never able to satisfy them completely.

"I'd advise others to stay out of your children's lives. Then maybe they'll want you more."

Julie is yearning for stability for her child. She's forever hopeful, often disappointed. Overinvolved, she has just a hint of, "If you don't intrude, you're wanted more." Julie has to see things as they are and back off until her child wants to welcome her into his life.

Parent Perspectives on Divorce and Grandparenting

Here are three divorced women with not-quite in-law situations. Some still have contact with their ex-mothers-in-law, some don't. This is how they answered the same questions:

• Bernadette said, "My children were married for twelve years, and recently separated. I'm no longer a mother-in-law, and I feel a void because I had a good relationship with my ex-daughter-in-law, and my ex-mother-in-law. My daughter-in-law still calls me 'Mom' when we talk, although that's rare because she hardly phones nowadays. When we are together, I don't get into the way she or my son live. Generally, we focus on the children's needs, and what they are doing in school. I hope at some future time we can have a casual friendship.

"When my son visits, he seems happy, and that makes me happy. I would like to see him in a contented marital situation in the future.

"The advice I'd give others is, Try not to be judgmental and stay away from personal questions."

"As far as my own ex-mother-in-law, I have many fond memories of the hours we spent together over the years — of wonderful times. She had her faults, but I let them go, because she was always there for me. When I divorced my husband after being married for over twenty-five years, although my mother-in-law and I remained close, there weren't many phone calls. My ex-mother-in-law wanted me to remarry, and when I didn't, she became closer to my ex-husband's new wife, a very compassionate and accommodating person.

"When I visited Florida, I used to see her, and that kept the relationship alive. She was always close to my children until the day she died. They loved her very much. I believe it's a good idea to have some kind of friendship with in-laws, even ex-in-laws — it sets an example for children and grandchildren. They learn that people can get along no matter what the circumstances."

Bernadette, very giving in spirit, really considers the people around her. She's taking an empathic stance, even though it may be hard to maintain a relationship with her not-quite-daughter-in-law because of her own child's conflicts with his ex-mate. This appears to be an example of positive resolution in a difficult situation.

• Sally said, "My husband's parents were divorced and remarried, so I had *two* mothers-in-law. Presently I am divorced. I send Mother's Day cards to my ex-husband's mother, Alice (we were married eleven years), and she and I are still close. I call her 'Mom' and speak to her on holidays and whenever I get a chance, and she calls me, too.

"In her mind I was always 'Fletcher's wife,' rather than 'Sally,' but in 1986, I had an automobile accident and almost died. Then we developed a close relationship. Before, I don't think she was aware of how she felt about me.

"I still feel this ex-mother-in-law is family, even though I'm divorced from her son. Alice is a good person, and I had a real sh—ty divorce, but my child has a loving relationship with this grandmother, and Alice has always been interested in my child's life, the same way she has been interested in mine.

"My ex-husband's father's wife, Eloise, on the other hand, was a different story. This person was sweet to your face, but not the real person. When we were married, we borrowed $1500 from her. My husband was in school then, and we needed the money for him to finish his education. Eloise was in agreement about lending it, but it seemed she wished to make us feel bad, because three months later, she started throwing the loan in our faces. She'd say, 'I won't have this money for my old age.'

"We repaid the loan in two years, exactly as we had promised.

When asked about how she handled the feelings she had, Sally answered, "I put my negative feelings about my in-laws aside, but every once in a while I would respond with anger. Then I'd feel spent, but not guilty, because I felt my anger was justified, and I always fought fair. I never told Eloise what I thought about her comments on the money we borrowed. Alice loaned us money, too. She never wanted it back."

"During the time my husband and I were married, Alice was married, and then separated for three years. Her husband was having an affair, and in her pain, Alice turned to me. We spent time on the phone regularly, and I gave her comfort. Then she reconciled with her husband, and lived with him until he died.

"When my husband left me, I reached out to Alice in the same kind of pain, and she responded. She came through for me as I had come through for her, and it made me feel loved and helped, and I value our relationship even more.

"Here's the advice I'd give others: Know how you feel. Don't allow yourself to be abused mentally, verbally, or in any other way. Speak up when you're not in accord. Say, 'I'm sorry you feel that way, but I disagree.' Know that you won't always succeed in making the other person understand. What is necessary is not succeeding, but that in attempting to make the other understand, you've done your best. If you're interested in being real, you must be able to say what you feel. It's better to focus on the positive, but be aware of the negative.

"Let me tell you one incident that stands out in particular. Alice, with her white skin, looked down at my infant son when he was born, and said, 'His skin is very fair. I hope he doesn't grow to be swarthy like you.'

"I laughed at her, because she's intelligent and bright, but misguided. That remark was really prejudicial, and all prejudice is stupidity, but my mother-in-law didn't have any awareness. She said something really foolish, but she wanted good things for me, so I was able to overlook a remark that could have been misconstrued. Because the relationship was so warm and caring, the remark was unimportant. I laughed instead, put it aside and focused on the positive."

Sally has a complicated set of relationships. However, mature in her outlook, she has overlooked insults, making a determination not to let them interfere with her relationships. Unlike people who hang on to slights, Sally wants to set a better example for her child. Instead of highlighting the critical, keeping the anger cooking, Sally chooses to emphasize the positive.

To a large degree, all of us create the emotional environment we live in. We have the choice to make it pleasant or miserable. As Drs. Gary McKay and Don Dinkmeyer say in their popular psychology book, *How You Feel Is Up To You!,* if we hold on to discord, it will radiate out, but if we choose harmony this, too, will provide a ripple effect.

• Sylvia said, "When my husband left me for another woman, I expected to continue the relationship with my mother-in-law. Whatever I had with her son had nothing to do with her, but minutes after the separation, she dropped me completely. I was always there for her whenever she needed to talk, and when she had surgery and wanted me with her, I was there, too.

"It follows I felt doubly abandoned — two daggers instead of one — which was extremely painful.

"Now joyous occasions become unpleasant. Stressful. I dread them. My children also feel a great loss, for Evelyn is their only grandmother, and they are angry because she totally pushed me out.

"I'd advise grandparents to keep up the relationship with your not-quite son/daughter-in-law — for the sake of the grandchildren if for no other reason — even if it's just a polite relationship. Otherwise, there are many unnecessary hurts, and the children get pulled apart."

Sylvia's not-quite-mother-in-law allowed her son's actions to control her own. She rejected her ex-daughter-in-law just as her son did. Sylvia alerts mothers-in-law to the pain they put on the grandchildren, who are getting pulled apart twice.

It will be hard for the grandchildren to maintain a relationship over time if Evelyn continues to avoid Sylvia. In the long run, it is Evelyn who has the most to lose. If she cares about her grandchildren, it will be worth her effort to maintain at least a polite relationship, despite difficulties.

Gay and Lesbian Lifestyles

In the fifties, if you were a young woman who didn't have a date on Saturday night, you never talked about it — but thoughts of spinsterhood flew through your head. I knew I had to be married by twenty. My grandmother said, "If you're not, you'll be an old maid."

Being an "old maid" was thought the worst thing that could happen to you and your parents. You pictured yourself in the future as the perennial caretaker — not quite part of the family, yet not alone — so it was better to be married to someone not exactly wonderful than to be single. Consequently, by the time I was in my late teens, I was committed to finding a mate, a fellow I could live with the rest of my life.

It was a coupled world then, as today, but society had more defined roles: the man was the breadwinner; the woman married, stayed home, and raised the children. To be part of the "in" group, we conformed, decorating ourselves internally to fit the values of friends and family — without exploring — and those values became absolute for us.

Most unmarried women in my day lived out their lives as second class citizens. People with alternative lifestyles, unable to deal with ostracism, "closeted" that side of themselves. Homosexuals were generally thought of as outcasts and labeled as "queers." Some people even believed homosexuality was contagious; there were those who thought that about cancer, too.

Most of the absolutes of the fifties have turned out not to be true, of course. Look at the single working woman. No longer an outcast, today she is known as a career person, and is widely accepted by many male business colleagues as an equal.

We're not out of the woods yet, but there has been movement.

"What Did I Do Wrong?

Although homosexuals have come out in significant numbers, discrimination abounds. And many not-quite in-laws feel guilty, as if some wrong turn they took in child-rearing were somehow responsible for their child's homosexuality. The anguish for both can be heartbreaking. Many parents ask, "What did I do wrong?"

The best information we have today says, "Nothing!"

Recent research, reported in medical journals and the popular press, suggests there is a link between sexual orientation and genetics. Your child's sexual identity may have little to do with his or her upbringing, and much to do with genes. If confirmed by further studies, these findings mean that neither you nor your child had any control over whether he or she is heterosexual or homosexual. While it is too early to draw firm conclusions, and some scientists are skeptical that a single gene would make the difference, it's time to stop judging — and misjudging — ourselves and our children.

Can You Deal with It?

We all know people with gay or lesbian lifestyles who are prominent, highly productive, funny, sensitive, kind, often creative individuals. They, like every one of us, cry out for acceptance and loving relationships with family members.

Maybe a time will come when we stop the gay-bashing, when we look beneath the surface, when we no longer project our emotional baggage onto others, when we back away from our modern witch hunts.

Parents of children whose lifestyles are other than they hoped (children in many cases who will not make them in-laws in the traditional sense) have to acknowledge that their offspring, like the rest of us, need approval and want support.

If you stepped into your child's shoes, what would you want him or her to say to you? Wouldn't it be "I accept you no matter what"? Children *are* supposed to be loved for their being, not for their doing.

If we want a successful relationship with our adult children we let go of "have to's," and acknowledge that our children's standards are often not our standards, and although we'd like them to reflect our thoughts, ideals, and values, they may not. We focus on the important things — that our child is successful in work, in love, in ways that matter to *him or her*," and if given a chance can only enhance our lives. Even if, at times, there's little to smile at and they make us cry, they are nonetheless our children.

When they were young and brought home friends of the same sex, we accepted those children, happy our youngster had someone to play with. We encouraged those relationships then. Why can't we do the same now, and allow their partners to enter our lives?

Yes, it means changing our own behavior and attitudes. And indeed it evokes anxiety, and days will not always be fair, but changing one's conduct may permit a not-quite in-law to open her home and heart and keep the family together.

It's not simple, because this isn't a role we as parents know, period. The role of mother-in-law is an "easier" process to go through, because you *had* a mother-in-law, and you *knew* mothers-in-law. The process of being not-quite an in-law is extremely complicated. It requires more courage and adjustment, but eventually you learn that every person has to march to his/her own drummer.

Some not-quite in-laws will have to broaden their perspectives, to open themselves to seeing the world with its infinite variety, each human being having a purpose, all beautiful, fragile, interesting, none better than another.

When I was a kid, a very overweight woman lived in the brownstone across from my family. Her ruddy face, shot with giant pores, had lines the vicissitudes of life had etched into it, lips streaked with red that smeared half-way through the day, and hair that had a mind of its own.

"*Dollink*," she'd call through the window, her accent spilling over like the pots of chicken paprikash she was always preparing, "I'm making your favorite tonight. Come for dinner."

And I would, for I was drawn to the love she offered, her sweetness, *joie de vivre,* the ability she had to make troubles evaporate like smoke on a windy day. Her humanity taught me to look beyond the exterior and reevaluate after a first glance.

That's what we have to do for our children — search deeper, and let them know they're okay. The year two thousand is just around the corner. Let's make it an opportunity to open our minds and hearts.

If your child is homosexual, and you're unhappy with the idea, then you'll have to grieve your losses. Obviously it's painful — however open our society professes to be, we are quite intolerant of some differences. There are steps you can take, a process you can go through, to get past the pain, with a professional if necessary.

Parent Perspectives on Gay and Lesbian Lifestyles

One way to begin to deal with these issues is to ask questions — of yourself, of your children, of others who share the experience. I asked parents to share their responses to these:*How has your child's lifestyle affected your life? What advice can you give to parents with a similar situation? What would you tell parents who say, "What did I do wrong?"*

• Janice said, "My first feelings and thoughts were shock and dismay. I kept it a secret, which was wrong, terrible of me, but it was what I was into — protecting. Actually, this made things worse. My son was in his twenties, and it was awful because my child was going through a lot of grief. I think he disbelieved his feelings, and that's what caused him to become a substance abuser.

"Once the family was told, we sought counseling.

"From the beginning, I was always there for my son and supported him without question. His lifestyle is on my mind a lot today, but being open is absolutely unburdening. I'm glad that he's met someone he cares about, and I think it's wonderful because I want my child to be happy. He'd like to bring his significant other home for Christmas, and that's fine with me now, but I don't know how I'll feel when the time comes."

When asked if there was anything she'd like to say to other parents that would be helpful, Janice answered, "I think every person is going to handle their situation in whatever way is comfortable for them."

Janice is still trying to work through the process and accept her feelings. When she can let go, she'll be able to move on to a more accepting place — and she won't have to miss out on the pleasure of being there for her child during her lifetime.

• Charles said, "There were three phases I went through. The first was disappointment. My immediate reaction when I found out that my son was gay was to find a psychiatrist to 'straighten him out.' Once, I got past the initial shock, I moved into phase two. I started reading books on the subject and realized my son was looking for acceptance.

"My wife adjusted faster, but I said things that were heartless, and for a while it was 'our secret.' Then somehow we entered phase three. Once we became more open, it was far easier to accept our child's lifestyle. We had a family dinner and he wanted to bring a friend, and we said, 'Okay.' That was another barrier broken.

"Now I realize what a warm, caring, sensitive person my son is. I see him as an 'open book,' and when I meet people today, I'm as comfortable talking about my son as I am about my other children, and I enjoy being with him. He's bright, clever, funny, and savvy politically. We have intelligent conversations.

"I think I will reach phase four. Right now this child is looking for a life mate. I hope he eventually finds one, and that the relationship will last.

"Phase four will be when I can deal with his talk of marriage. To me, this is still something only men and women do, and it bothers me to see two guys with their arms around each other.

"The advice I'd offer is: Understand this child did not choose to be the way he or she is. Once you understand this was not a choice, then you can deal with him or her. Remember this is your child, so give them your empathy. They go through hell. And where is the first place they should get support? Isn't it from parents and siblings?

"Most of all know that your child is not rejecting you or your values. Your child loves you, so keep talking and caring and being together when you can.

Charles seems open to growth and has allowed himself to adapt. Foremost was the love of his child, so he did what was necessary to maintain the relationship and work through his disappointment.

• Tamara said, "There is the initial shock. I was a little surprised when my son, Frank, told me. Then I said, 'Hey, everyone has to live their own life.' Frank's my son. If you accept your child you accept their lifestyle. This didn't change my feelings for him, and I like his significant other. He's nice. Now I have two friends.

"Because of my acceptance of him, my son's friend has become close to his family."

This appears to be an example of healthy resolution. Tamara wants to keep the relationship with her son and that's what she's focused on.

• Angela said, "It was a shock. I was very upset, confused as to why, but never angry. Joe was in his twenties, in college, when my husband and I found out. We'd never had an inkling before. My husband felt more responsible, and thought if he had been a macho-man, this wouldn't have happened.

"My son is a bright, kind, wonderful person. Everyone loves Joe. When I found out about his homosexuality, I did a lot of reading. I don't blame myself. I did the best I could. My son talks about how lucky he is to have the kind of parents he has.

"Joe's forty-six now, a professional, and has a friend he's been living with for twenty years. It's been a good relationship. I like my son's significant other, he's a fine man. I even met his parents. I'm happy Joe's with one person, so there's no concern with AIDS, and his relationship is like a marriage. What bothers me is I won't have grandchildren, and this bothers Joe, too. His friend donated sperm to a lady friend, and now has a child which he visits, but my son has never considered doing this.

"The advice I'd give others is: Love your child and don't feel guilty. Above all, don't pussyfoot around the subject of homosexuality. Tell your friends about your child — tell everybody."

Angela's advice to talk openly is sound, because secrets poison a relationship. She's struggled with guilt, but she also did the work needed to bring her to acceptance and to maintain a loving relationship with her son.

• Lucy said, "It was painful when I first learned my daughter, Joanna, was a lesbian. I went through lots of guilt because 'the mother is to blame for everything,' and I blamed myself. It took me time to understand. Then I was able to say 'Stop! You have a certain amount of power, but you don't have *that much* power.'

"I realized Joanna hadn't changed. The romantic image in my head had, so I had to grieve the death of the person I thought was my daughter, to have her reborn to me as the person she is.

"Keeping secrets corrupts a relationship, because there is so much to cover up you can never get close. Of course, when you tell others, there is always a risk, so you protect yourself and your child as best you can. There will always be some who will judge you, but that can't be helped.

"Joanna is still the warm, caring person she always was. I didn't have to read a million books on the topic, but I had to deal with my emotions.

"Today we have a wonderful relationship, and she's close with everyone. We didn't lose our sense of being a family. My husband and I enjoy being with our children and have accepted Joanna's significant other, even include her in our celebrations.

"My daughter's lifestyle has opened up my world and helped me see things from a different point of view. I feel parents can learn from children the same way children learn from parents.

"I'm concerned about her being rejected by the world — by people who make assumptions concerning behavior they know little about.

"To parents who say 'What did I do wrong?' You didn't do anything wrong. Things happen over which you have no control. The advice I'd give: Stay connected to your children. And make your child's significant other as comfortable as possible."

Lucy has grieved who she thought her daughter was and allowed new possibilities to come in, letting her daughter's lifestyle be enhancing to the family. Here is a woman who sees the glass as half-full rather than the other way around.

Adult Children's Perspectives on Gay and Lesbian Lifestyles

I learned a great deal from asking questions of adult children in gay and lesbian relationships: *How has your gay/lesbian lifestyle affected your life? What was the impact on your family? What advice can you give to parents? How can you help them understand?*

• Kim said, "My parents wish I were a more traditional person and had a man. I accept that this relationship is something they're not happy about. My parents have never discussed my homosexuality with anyone. They are ashamed and embarrassed, and I'm sorry about that. It leaves them alone at times.

"My mother feels it's her fault. If she could get out of 'Poor me,' and consider the people she loves, and stop thinking 'How can you do this?' she might be able to get into my feelings.

"I know it can't be easy for my parents. It takes time for people to react and respond. They have to say to themselves, 'This is the way my child is. It's not what I thought it would be.' But no one plans this. No one plans on kids moving away. No one plans on illness, either. Some things just happen.

"My parents can't deny I'm a happier person, and I've let them know I appreciate what they've done for me. I'm more accepting now than when I was twenty-three. The values I have and the things I'm concerned about, I acquired from my parents. They taught me to care about others.

"I don't know if you ever get away from wanting to please parents. I wish I could be the person they would have liked. Their "right things"are not "right" for me. Sometimes I wish it would be different, and I would have their approval.

"I've never talked to my parents about marriage with my partner. I wish they were more appreciative of her — she's always there for me, and generous of spirit. Once, she went to hug my mother. My mother stuck her hand out.

"I know they're glad my partner's there, they don't want me to be alone, but I can't change their minds about this relationship, so it's pointless to argue. I'm not willing to make my parents unhappy.

"They are older people, set in their ways. Insecure. They're probably doing the best they can. In their hearts they are tied to what they grew up with, and I'm still intimidated by them. My father's silences makes me feel terrible.

"Advice I'd give parents: Explore the issues instead of shoving them under the rug. Then, try to get beyond your own pain, so you can understand others. Get into your child's feelings. It can't be easy for them."

Kim can't be close with her parents because her parents refuse to talk about her lesbianism. They remain stuck in their initial reactions — the mother blaming herself, and the father locking his feelings inside where they sit and fester — and Kim is trying to come to terms with their rigidity and disappointment and at the same time get on with her own life.

Consider, is a prejudice against homosexuality really more valuable to you than a relationship with your child?

• Rick said, "I'm more open-minded and accepting than most straight people I know. When it comes to God, originally I thought I had committed a sin. But I'm not doing anything wrong. This is how God created me, and it's okay. I know deep down in my heart God loves me for who I am because this is who he wanted me to be.

"It's difficult living in a world where you're not wanted. Everything is against you when you're gay — you're discriminated against, you're the butt of jokes, and somehow it's okay.

"I felt alone in the world as a teenager. It's a struggle to be okay with being gay. I wonder about everything because I'm thinking about it all the time, trying to find answers. In the final analysis, it's about are you okay with yourself. We all go through this, but a gay person is forced into it at a different stage of life.

"My parents have come a long way. Originally, my mother didn't talk to me and didn't want to meet my friends. She doesn't want to be seen in public with her gay son and his friend. Now, she is trying, but she doesn't accept me totally — not like she accepts my siblings. I had no problem with them. I'm bringing a friend home in a few weeks, but my parents don't take my relationship seriously. I believe I'll always be considered different.

"My advice to parents: Don't blame your children for who they are. Being gay or straight shouldn't be an issue — it's like having blue or brown eyes, you don't have a choice. Parents should be concerned that their children are good people, that they don't hurt others, that they are considerate and loving, people who make a living and are able to take care of themselves. Accept me and my friends.

"I feel my significant other is like any in-law. Not allowing him to be included in family celebrations is like saying to a married brother, 'You're welcome, but your wife isn't.'

"I've always been a good person, and I allow my parents to say what they wish, but I lead my own life. It's telling myself, 'I'm okay.' I can't be frustrated any longer or try to make it different. I hope my parents understand."

Rick shows us how difficult the struggle is to be gay in our society. He's trying to maintain his faith in God, while dealing with rejection, and vividly portrays what a young person has to go through. It hasn't been easy for Rick to feel good about himself, and you hear the struggle in his words as he tries to feel okay. Like all children, Rick has never stopped wanting the approval of his parents.

• Jeremy said, "I think I'm a better person for being gay. Once I accepted it with the help of therapy, it opened up my potential. I feel a certain amount of freedom, and can express more without fear. I can go to a baseball game as well as the ballet and love them both.

"I told my folks when I was in my thirties. My mother cried when she found out, but my parents' support has been incredible. They are straight-arrow, self-made people but they say, 'As long as you're happy, we're happy!' If they had a problem with my being gay, they never told me. I'm the same child they always loved. And they always welcome anyone I bring home for a visit.

"I've always felt cared about. My whole life everything was 'soft and comfy' like being wrapped in fur.

"My parents didn't do anything wrong. Being gay is like a blood type. You don't get to choose it. This is where education is important. My friends are bright and aware, and feel free to discuss things. Like seeks like.

"There's a part of me that adores children and would like to be a father, but another part says, 'No way in hell!' Luckily, my parents have grandchildren from another child. But one of the things I worry about is living alone when I get old. Another thing is the bigotry out there, because I know prejudice comes from ignorance. No one chooses to be different, and if given a choice, you prefer to blend in."

Homosexuality has given Jeremy a certain amount of freedom. In touch with his own androgyny, he is as comfortable with both his male and female side, and this gives him a great deal of pleasure.

• Cheryl said, "My parents can't seem to develop a way of looking at my significant other like a real spouse. They ignore my partner. Even on the phone they don't chat, just use my significant other as an answering machine. They also exclude her from formal occasions, and I want my parents to treat my partner just like any of their other children's spouses — or as close to it as possible. If we feel okay about our lifestyle, parents have to abide by it or lose the relationship. They may not like my mate, but as in a heterosexual lifestyle, they have to accept her because she's the one I've chosen to live with for the rest of my life.

"Many parents with alternative lifestyle children have to go through a period of mourning. They have to grieve what they had hoped for, and deal with AIDS and discrimination. *We*, too, have to deal with discrimination, AIDS, loss of jobs, people thinking us sick or immoral, and not accepting us for whom we are. My father's concern was, would it be too hard for me.

"Generally speaking, parents feel they will be embarrassed — humiliated. They question, 'Where did I go wrong?'

"The answer psychology tells us is that homosexuality has little to do with parents. Therefore, parents should not blame themselves for their children's lifestyles.

"It's not only the parents who are dealing with strong feelings, but the child, too. Both are struggling to get through life with a different set of rules.

"A helpful suggestion is to stop wondering what people do in the privacy of their bedroom, because that's such a minute part of the relationship. Often people don't see the individual, but focus on the sexuality — their minds wander where it doesn't belong. Forget about the sex. The bedroom is a very private place.

"Another suggestion, join a support group where you can go with or without your child, to talk about frustrations. PFLAG (Parents & Friends Of Lesbians & Gays) is one organization throughout the country.

"Let your child know your love hasn't changed because of his/her homosexuality. Don't explain things away with 'She's going through a phase' or 'Going to therapy.' and ask, 'Are you cured yet?'

"Crisis often produces growth, and in many families this is a crisis. After grieving their losses, parents may have to forgive their child. This doesn't mean that the child needs forgiveness, but it might be helpful for the parents to go through the process, to let go of *their* needs and realize their child is a separate individual. Your offspring is going through a mourning process, too. Both may be going through it simultaneously.

"Parents have to juggle a lot, but if they aren't really accepting of their child, that's the message they put out — rejection.

"Homosexuality isn't a choice. I understand every parent's wish without question, and I mourn with them, but they have to remind themselves that their child is not less bright or funny, so why throw away the good stuff?"

Cheryl illustrates that lack of acceptance causes pain. Most parents don't want to hurt their children, but negating a partner is a continuation of estrangement. This deeply compassionate woman also reminds us to be cognizant of where your mind is going — to see if it's on the right route. It's helpful, too, she says, "For the child to understand the parent's pain."

Maybe this calls for parents to express feelings without blaming. If we have a wound on a physical level, we know it needs tending, so we cleanse it, then healing can take place. Cheryl suggests you talk about your wounds, mourn your losses, and move beyond the deepest pain. The pain may never be *totally* removed, but it doesn't have to be as pervasive as it was in the beginning, and eventually, you'll get in touch with good feelings, and be able to work toward a satisfying relationship.

Minding Your Family

Given a choice, all parents of children with non-traditional lifestyles (with all the vulnerabilities such lifestyles imply) want a warm, loving enduring relationship with their children. Still, they have to deal with their own inner turmoil and disappointments.

None of the children I talked with remotely considered blaming their parents, though the parents, in many instances, blame themselves. Nor did the children "choose" homosexuality; *it chose them*. These parents have to accept that fact and set an example of acceptance; move forward with open minds and caring hearts, acknowledging that they will not be "in-laws" in the traditional sense.

If you were to ponder losing your child in some way through an accident, or a fatal illness, for instance — would you be able to accept it? Most of us would say, "Of course not!"

So why throw away a living, loving, vital child because of a different lifestyle? We love our children, and can always create room for another presence in our lives. What really matters is *keeping the family together*.

"*The mind*," says Milton, "*is it's own place, and in itself*
  Can make a heav'n of hell, a hell of heav'n."
What is your choice going to be?

You've travelled several hundred miles to visit your gay son and meet his partner for the first time. As you discuss plans to go out to dinner, you find your self uncomfortable about being out in public with an openly homosexual couple. You deal with the situation by saying,

    a. "Actually, I'd be just as happy eating dinner here in your apartment."

    b. "Do you have a favorite cafe that caters to... people like you?"

    c. "Are the restaurants around here pretty liberal?"

    d. "I'm a little uncomfortable about going out. Can we talk about it?"

    e. "It must be tough to find a place where you're comfortable eating out."

What's the meaning of this?

    a. Maybe it's time to be up-front with your son. Tell him you'd be embarrassed to be out in public with him and his friend..

    b. Are you saying you'd feel ok as long as the crowd was compatible?

    c. Afraid they'll throw you out?

    d. Congratulations! You're on the road to opening communication with your son and his partner.

    e. This may be an understanding comment, but probably still reflects your own discomfort.

Chapter 6

BRIDGING THE
COMMUNICATION GAP
The Other Mother's Guide
to When and How to Speak Up
...or Shut Up

*I*n this chapter, we're going to consider the topic that may well be the most complex of human activities.

Communication is basic to relationships, of course, essential for establishing bonds, and critical in understanding people better. Yet we rarely think about it unless someone else brings it up (that's happening with you right now as you read this chapter) or there's a problem in a relationship because communication has broken down.

Good communication skills are necessary in order to comprehend and respect another person's feelings, ideas, and values. Good skills allow you to show acceptance of another, even as you express dissatisfaction with the way that person *acts*. You can learn to use words effectively to get what you want without blaming. You can say what you need to say while respecting the other person's feelings. Good communication skills allow you to make good things happen!

The best way to build rapport with your children and to prevent verbal fireworks is to communicate *skillfully*. The suggestions in this chapter can help you do that.

Like most folks, you assume without thinking about it that your meanings are received by others when you speak. But it often takes much more than a few words to convey what one really has in mind. Effective communication means talking and relating in ways that get your thoughts, feelings, and needs across to others clearly, and — whenever possible — without hurting anyone.

One point was made again and again by the people I interviewed for this book: *we could all benefit from learning how to communicate better!*

Communication is the process of putting thoughts and feelings together to formulate ideas and transfer information. Thoughts, feelings, and intentions are conveyed through words, body language, and tone of voice, and — if the sender is to make the point — must be sent without creating defensiveness and uncertainty in the listener.

We're all unique and imperfect, of course, and so is the language we speak. So we run into trouble expressing ourselves. No wonder we sometimes feel the people we're closest to don't understand what we mean, and that they don't do what we expect them to. Instead, they irritate us, and we irritate them. If we irritate our in-law children too much, we push them away, and if we lose them, we may lose our own children, and our grandchildren as well.

How can you avoid that risk?

There are two major steps. The first is to *overcome some of the barriers* to good communication — things you may do without thinking that get in the way of your best intentions. The second is to *build good communication skills* of your own. The rest of this chapter is devoted to helping you get started on both steps.

Communication Barrier #1: Magical Thinking

I'm sure you've asked yourself many times, when spoken to, "I wonder what he or she means?" This is because the intention wasn't obvious. One key cause of communication problems is that we sometimes entertain a fantasy that the other person will know what we need and provide it. That is magical thinking, a childhood belief that wishing will make it so. And when our listeners don't come through, we're unhappy. So the lesson here is, *say what you mean*, clearly, and straightforwardly to prevent feelings of frustration, confusion, resentment, and disappointment.

Let's explore a typical situation.

Mother-in-law Margaret: *"Have you given any thought to the holidays?"* (What Margaret really wants is an invitation to her children's home. She's tired of cooking and would like to be a guest this time. She's hoping — magical thinking — that her unspoken meaning will be *interpreted* and she'll be invited.)

Daughter-in-law: *"Not really. It's several weeks away."*

This mother-in-law has danced around the topic, hoping to get the response she wanted. The daughter-in-law doesn't do anything wrong. She has merely answered the question asked. She doesn't realize there was a hidden meaning to the inquiry because Margaret isn't straightforward.

Being direct is scary for some women, because we were trained to be "nice" — and manipulative — rather than candid. She may come away from the interaction feeling hurt and undervalued, wondering if she'll *always* be the one in the kitchen.

It's possible, too, that she will accumulate these hurt and undervalued feelings. She'll collect them like spare change, and, when she has amassed enough feelings of being unappreciated, she may decide to cash them in by distancing herself from her daughter-in-law, or dumping all the bad feelings at once. Alas, her in-law child hasn't a clue about what's happening.

Some people cash in their anger coins a few at a time by carrying a grudge, always casting their adult children in a negative light. For instance, when someone asks, "How's your son/daughter-in-law?" this type of mother-in-law may roll her eyes and think, *"Look who we're talking about."*

Others carry around feelings of resentment for years, reinforcing their belief that they're right about the person in question. Then they feel justified when they cash in big, by, say, not talking to their in-law child. More importantly they lose sight of their losses. The act of cashing in feels good for the moment, but in reality you lose much more than you gain. Excluding an in-law child could cause the loss of your natural child and your grandchildren. Relationships become estranged, and there is a general deterioration of the family unit.

Here's a healthier approach. Ask yourself:

- What's my goal?
- What are the consequences of my actions?
- What will I lose?
- How long will I feel good with these losses?

When most angry or hurt, try hard to focus on what's good about the other person. Isn't having your family intact more important than an accumulation of hurts? The lesson here is, to avoid collecting ill feelings, learn to express clearly what you want.

Magical thinking easily leads to a very common — and dangerous — assumption about the ability of others to recognize our needs. You may believe — as many people unfortunately do — that people who love you know what you mean, need, and want. So you hide your feelings.

Margaret expected her daughter-in-law to pick up on *unexpressed thoughts*, which is where she failed. Here's an approach that might work better. We'll replay the scene, this time with straight talk. (More about straight talk later in this chapter.)

Mother-in-law Margaret: *"The holiday is in a few weeks. I'm very tired of doing all the preparations. I wonder if you and Jim would like to cook dinner this year?"*

Daughter-in-law: *"It sounds like you've had it with being the hostess. I haven't given it much thought, because it's several weeks away, but I'll think about it, and talk it over with Jim. Okay if I get back to you tomorrow?"*

By making a genuine effort to clearly spell out what she wanted, Margaret will now feel heard. Furthermore, she'll know that, even if her needs can't be met, they will be considered.

Communication Barrier #2: The Blame Game

Whether your son or daughter is a recent newlywed or your children have been married for a number of years, you know they see situations in a different light than you. This is especially true if their spouses were raised in another culture or religion, with other sensitivities and prejudices. The histories that shaped them can build barriers. A blaming game full of ill will can easily arise if there is a lack of understanding.

Even though no one likes to be on the receiving end of blame, somehow we can all dish it out. Conversations are full of "She always says...," "He never answers me," and "Nobody cares!" Indeed, we all know how to blame, but the usual result is that it simply damages the relationship. Blaming has a boomerang effect. It comes back to hit you in the face.

Again we want to replace blame with understanding. Consider the rule *you get what you give*. If you want good relationships with your in-law children, try to let go of the criticism. Learn to *"accentuate the positive."*

Suzette Haden Elgin, in *The Gentle Art of Verbal Self Defense,* points out that "Blamers pepper their speech with words like these: *always, never, nothing, nobody, everything, none, at once.* When they ask questions (and they ask far too many questions) they put an abnormally heavy stress on the question word. 'WHY did you do that?' 'WHAT is the MATTER with you?' 'WHEN did you ever consider the feelings of ANYbody except yourself?'" Elgin goes on to say blamers make a person feel threatened as they scowl, raise their voices, even shake a finger, not realizing how they come across.

If you recognize yourself as a blamer — a fault-finding mother-in-law — think about how you dislike it when others criticize *you*.

Take Isabel, for example. One fine Saturday, she stops by to visit her children and spend time with the grandchildren. She finds her daughter out shopping, her son-in-law Doug at his desk working on tax returns, and her grandchildren in front of the television set. A few moments after saying "Hello," Isabel complains.

Isabel: *"They're always watching television. It's not good for their eyes, Doug. They should be outside playing."*

Doug: *They were outside all morning."*

Doug feels attacked and hears Isabel's words as criticism of his parenting efforts, because the children *are* in front of the television set, so he responds defensively. Even if Isabel means well, Doug will view his mother-in-law as interfering, and by implying she knows better how to raise the children, Isabel is undermining the relationship between herself and her children.

This mother-in-law has to stop finding fault and remind herself that her children have a right to raise their children any way they please. She doesn't know everything (she assumed the children were in all day, when in fact, they weren't). The job of a mother-in-law is neither to correct nor criticize, it is to support, and the job of a grandmother is to *enjoy* her grandchildren.

Let's look at Ava. Her son-in-law, Craig said, "She was a little lady with nice eyes — an unpretentious person, very supportive, who didn't beat around the bush. Ava did everything for her kids except breathe for them. They were her life, and when I married into the family, I, too, became part of her inner circle.

"One day, upset with my boss, I was talking to Ava about the situation at work, and she, who didn't know from mincing words, said, 'Don't let people bother you. They all sit on the toilet and squeeze the same way.'"

Ava knew how to support her son-in-law. Her basic message says it all: *I love you* — you're as good as anyone else, no matter who he is. How lucky to have an Ava rather than an Isabel as one's mother-in-law. Which would you rather be?

I'm sure you can come up with dozens of other things we do to get in our own way and make communication difficult. Still, if you can overcome your own *magical thinking* and *blame game* behaviors, you're well on your way to being a better communicator — and a better mother-in-law.

Now let's examine a number of practical strategies you can use —- starting today —- to *enhance* your effectiveness in communication with those you care about.

Communication Enhancer #1: Listening

Listening is easy, isn't it? Your ears work, and you hear what others are saying, so it's no trick to listen. Or is it?

Unfortunately, to truly listen to another person is not easy. Nor is listening automatic. It takes time and effort. It means putting your needs away for the moment. When it's important to listen, you have to stop what you are doing and pay attention, or you won't hear everything.

Forget what your kids told you about studying in front of the TV, or while they played loud rock music. It's only possible to actively focus on one thing at a time. If you intend to listen to someone, you'll need to concentrate with genuine interest on what the other person is saying. If you don't really listen, whatever the other person says won't make a dent. You will miss important information and, five minutes later, say, "She said *what...*?"

A good listener has to let speakers reveal in detail what they want to get across — without passing judgement — or else the listening won't work. The most important thing a good listener has to do is *hear*.

You never really hear what another is saying if your mind is occupied with your own thoughts — even when those thoughts are focussed on how you intend to respond. Unless evaluation and judgement are set aside, you tend to hear what you want to, rather than what is actually said. That's not receiving the information being sent, that's only processing what your brain *thinks* you heard. Consequently, you don't respond in a way that is constructive to the other person or yourself.

You may find listening easier on the telephone, because there are fewer distractions present. It's a good way to practice your listening skills. If it helps, you can always hold a paper in front of you that says:

- Listen
- *Do Not Interrupt!*
- Clarify
- Listen
- *Do Not Advise!*
- Listen
- Feedback
- Listen

This is what listening is about. It does *not* mean *fixing* someone else's problem. It does not mean offering solutions, *unless* you're asked, "What are your thoughts?", "What would you do?", or "Any ideas?"

Listening means trying to think what would help the other person — putting yourself in the speaker's shoes. It doesn't mean being in agreement, but it does mean hearing the speaker's message: verbal, nonverbal, and emotional.

In any case, by listening carefully — and that means your brain is cleared of all other concerns — you have an opportunity to hear feelings expressed. In doing so, both mother-in-law and son or daughter-in-law can grow to understand each other and enhance their relationship.

Listening is the magic ingredient in communication. In fact, it is the *chief* ingredient in communication. Listening helps raise consciousness, promotes autonomy, and makes more rewarding personal relationships. In this era of hurry-up rush-rush, you can't believe how much a good listener is appreciated.

Maybe you've noticed how difficult it is to shut off the voices inside your head when someone else is speaking — voices that tell you *"pick up Harry's poison ivy medicine,"* or *"get to the bank before three."* (You may even be hearing them while reading this book.) It's hard to blank out what's in your brain, not have other thoughts interfere. When listening to others, many individuals keep their inner tape going while trying to help with a fast fix. Given the tempo of our modern lives, they're usually in a rush to jump in and offer advice, with "You should..." grabbing the focus away from the speaker. They believe they are being helpful. They're not.

Offering unasked advice, even well-meant advice, is a put-down, and when you tell another what to do, it causes pain. The implied message is that the other doesn't know how to do it, that you know better. But that's not want you want to get across.

The reply you receive might be, "Yes, you're right," but at this point, you may notice your in-law child withdraw or change the topic. Accept your child's spouse by learning to listen and ask questions. "How" and "what" questions are best. For example:

- *"How else could that have been handled?"*
- *"How do you feel about it?"*
- *"What do you want to do now?"*
- *"What concerns you the most?"*
- *"What would make you happy?"*
- *"What would be best for you in this situation?"*
- *"How can I help you?"*

A listener has to hear information given and use feedback the way a fine camera brings into focus the important details of a picture. To make sure you heard correctly, *always* check the information received. Say, "Is this what you mean?" Then pay attention without expressing your feelings.

The thing you want to do is allow the other person to get the feelings out. If he or she is having a difficult time and asks for help, then you may communicate your thoughts with *"Have you thought about ...?"*

You can tell a lot by observing someone. For instance, if you watch a person's face carefully, you will recognize how he or she responds to moods and feelings. Good listeners are able to pick up on subtle nuances and analyze nonverbal signals. But even they can be fooled: Expressions such as smiles and tears may *seem* easy to read, but people often put on a happy face when there is no happiness, and when they cry, we can't be sure if the tears are of joy, sorrow or frustration.

A lot of what human beings do involves repeating what they learned at home when they were growing up — whether it's not to fall apart in front of others, or to put on a smiling face. If you pick up nonverbal signals that don't feel right, check them out, because good communication means accepting what another feels, and being supportive. When you are aware of something being wrong, you can always say, "I sense that something is upsetting you," and wait for an answer.

Suppose a mother-in-law forgets to acknowledge her daughter-in-law's birthday. While talking to the younger woman, she feels something remiss in the conversation.

Mother-in-law: *"It sounds like you're upset with me."*

Daughter-in-law: *"I am. You didn't even bother to send me a birthday card this year."*

The mother-in-law could respond, "I'm so sorry. It totally slipped my mind, and I apologize." And if she really wants to please her daughter-in-law, she could, in addition, send a belated birthday card.

If she values their relationship and wants "good things" to happen, she *won't* criticize, "Oh, you make such a big deal over nothing." Even if she is inclined to believe birthday cards are silly things to get upset about, she is wise to keep such thoughts to herself, and send a birthday card the next time.

Communication Enhancer #2: Straight Talk

Straight talk means saying something in a way that doesn't leave your intentions vague, so that you let the other person know exactly what you want. It's being up front, but sensitive, too. You describe *behaviors* rather than *character* flaws and you don't make assumptions. That way you have a good chance of getting your needs met.

Every time you send a message to someone, you want something back — an answer to a question, or for the other person to listen to you without advice or criticism, perhaps just to be understood. The listeners have to translate the message they hear, to process the words and feelings and be able to determine the intention.

Consequently, the response you get after sending your message is sometimes exactly what you were looking for, and sometimes it's not. The listener cannot meet your needs if your message isn't clear. When you find your listener confused, it is possible that your tone of voice, body language, and facial expressions don't mesh with the words he or she is hearing: something as simple as a shrug sends a message.

Communication Enhancer #3: Non-Verbal Signals

Tone of Voice. It's critically important for us mothers-in-law to be aware of our *tone* of voice. Tone is more than mere background music to words. Gentle words spoken stridently send a mixed message at the very least. Consequently, you fail to reach your audience, because the meaning comes across in your tone, not in the words themselves.

Body Language. Much of the message is conveyed by such key non-verbal cues as facial expression, gestures, body posture, eye contact. If you're really angry with someone, it doesn't come across very clearly if you say so with a big smile. If you say "I really care about you" with a sneer or with your back turned, your words are lost in the unspoken language of the body.

If you sincerely want to improve your communication, you'll have to pay as much attention to *how* you say things as you do to *what* you say. Practice with a mirror or tape recorder if you need to, to make sure your total message comes across just the way you want it to.

If nonverbal cues don't match the words, several things happen. First, people might be turned off to the relationship. Second, they will become confused because of the double messages. Since words, feelings, facial expressions, and body language all contribute to the meaning of a message, if they are not parallel, the person receiving them may wonder what's happening and how to respond.

While almost everyone thinks communication has to do with ears, it also has a great deal to do with eyes. Some psychologists suggest that how well you maintain eye contact may show how much you value a relationship.

Communication Enhancer #4: Be Specific

How many times has someone said to you off-handedly, "We have to get together. When you're in the neighborhood, I want you to drop in."

The words sound fine, but in order to really understand the meaning of this statement you have to consider the feelings behind it. Maybe this person truly wants to see you, and maybe not. The declaration alone doesn't get its *intention* across. The true message might just be: *I'm a nice person and don't want to offend, so I'll be polite and say the right thing. But don't bother calling — I'm really not interested.*

On the other hand, the message may mean: *I know you're in the neighborhood occasionally, and I'd feel hurt if you didn't visit me.* The listener will have to decipher the intention behind the words.

By not clearly identifying what you want in an interaction, you can cause yourself problems: Here is a mother-in-law (it could also be a daughter-in-law) who may want to know any number of things, but she isn't likely to get her needs met, because she wasn't forthright:

Mother-in-law Maria: *"Are you going shopping tomorrow?"*

Daughter-in-law Dolores: *"Yes. Isn't the weather lovely?"*

The trouble is that "Yes," period, was not the answer the mother-in-law was looking for. Often a message has a hidden agenda. Maria may really want to know:

- *What are you going to buy?*
- *Is my granddaughter going with you?*
- *Can you pick something up for me?*

However, she doesn't ask any of the above. Instead, she asks a *yes-or-no* question. Yes-or-no questions *stop* communication. Since the response is a mere affirmation and the topic changes, it's likely that it's finished with unless brought up again. This mother-in-law probably will not get her needs met. It seems she is afraid to ask for what she wants.

What does she really have in mind: information about shopping activities or a way of meeting her own needs? It never comes through. *Nor will it*, unless Dolores observes her mother-in-law better to pull out the underlying message, or Maria reframes the question in one of the following straight-talk ways:

- *"I haven't been to the stores for a while, and if you're going shopping tomorrow, I'd like to join you."*
- *"I have a free afternoon and I'd really like to get out of the house."*
- *"If Carla is going shopping with you tomorrow, would it be all right if I came, too?"*
- *"Since you're planning to be in the department stores tomorrow, would you pick up some bath towels for me that are on sale?"*

But Maria has never learned how to express her wants skillfully; she doesn't say what she means in a straightforward manner. Often, that is one of the traps people fall into when communicating. Whatever you say, you have a better chance of getting your needs met and avoiding problems if you reprogram yourself to be specific.

Communication Enhancer #5: Feeling Talk

Feelings are a critical element in messages and expressing them is a form of straight talk. All of us have varying feelings in any interaction with another, which can shift depending on the conversation. When we think of communication, we think first of "speakers" and "listeners," but let's factor in that other component — feelings. When we declare our feelings, we share an intimate part of ourselves, allowing others to see us as we really are. Moreover, we allow ourselves to be *vulnerable,* for there are risks to stripping away the protective public mask we usually wear — but in exchange we become richer emotionally.

You know what *you* feel — if you know yourself well — but you don't know what *the other person* feels. We don't always understand each other, because we don't come from the same set of life experiences; each of us is the product of a unique past history. Consequently, *you can never assume that other people feel the same as you.*

Yet, when we don't get clear information, often this is exactly what we do. We fill in the blanks based on our assumptions. Watch out! This can get you into trouble. If you assume, you may discover the truth of an old saying: "To *ass\u\me* makes an *ass* out of *you* and *me.*"

To avoid falling into that trap, don't jump to conclusions. It's best to clarify, then clarify some more. Ask questions. Then rephrase the other person's words to be sure you understood what you heard, and feed the information back to the speaker. This will save you grief later.

One simple statement may trigger varying feelings in different people. In fact, how we perceive a statement is generally aligned with our past experience.

Here's a situation in which a mother-in-law — Millie — has six married children. She telephones each and says, "The family is being invited to Cousin Jennifer's wedding in Florida. We can visit Disney World while we're there. Aunt Bea said she'll be happy to arrange hotel accommodations. So I told her, 'Go ahead.' Isn't that exciting?"

She talks on, filled with happy visions of a family reunion. Because she is elated with her invitation, this mother-in-law innocently *assumes* everyone else will feel the same. But communication is not a one-way street. It's a two way interaction. In this case the mother-in-law has made a big mistake by not checking out the feelings of her in-law children to determine their emotional response to the wedding invitation. She makes the assumption that, if she likes something, everyone else will, too.

In fact:

• Son-in-law Joe feels excited, because he likes Cousin Jennifer. Also, he has vacation time coming and his family always wanted to visit Disney World. This is a perfect opportunity to do both.

• Son-in-law Tom feels annoyed, because he had special plans for that weekend and will have difficulty changing them.

• Daughter-in-law Carol feels frustrated, because, although she'd like to go, she has a financial problem. She is expecting a baby in four months and the wedding expense will eradicate whatever she's saved toward nursery furniture.

• Daughter-in-law Mai hates Florida. She is scheduled to attend a professional meeting in Chicago that week, and had planned to visit friends on the weekend.

• Daughter-in-law Sue feels angry. She dislikes Cousin Jennifer. They never got along, and she doesn't want to attend the wedding.

• Daughter-in-law Christina feels guilty, because she couldn't afford to invite Cousin Jennifer to her own wedding.

This mother-in-law hasn't a clue that each couple feels different about the wedding trip. Notice, too, that the event has triggered a lot of unresolved feelings with unclear consequences. One may be that the younger people feel manipulated by the older one, because each wants to control his/her *own* destiny.

The bottom line is that you can't read another's mind. Everyone has their own agenda. The best thing would have been for the

The bottom line is that you can't read another's mind. Everyone has their own agenda. The best thing would have been for the mother-in-law to take the lead and let the children verbalize their feelings (some were pretty intense) about attending the wedding. Then she could also ask some questions. For example:

- *"What did you think when you received your invitation?"*
- *"How do you feel about going to Florida?"*
- *"How hard would it be for you financially?"*
- *"Do you want to talk it over with your spouse and get back to me?"*
- *"What can I do to help you?"*

By carefully considering the responses, Millie would not only increase her understanding of each of her children's and in-law children's feelings and needs, but establish a more open and empathetic relationship with them. But she would have to know how to *listen first*.

After listening to Carol's concerns about the wedding/vacation trip, Millie might reply, "You're saying the timing isn't right for you, and that money is tight now. But if the pregnancy is not so far along that there's a problem about traveling, would you really like to go if you could afford it?"

By listening, clarifying what she heard, then feeding back the information and talking openly, Millie would be able to understand her daughter-in-law's feelings and her needs.

If Millie had listened to her children, she would have had more insight into their lives and their options. She could then decide if she wanted to help them solve their dilemma, and how. She could:

- lend her children money
- give the trip as an anniversary gift
- offer a sympathetic ear — just show interest
- understand that not everyone has the same interests in relatives.

Communication Enhancer #6: "I-Messages"

Most of us don't feel comfortable revealing our feelings. But if we want to be close to someone, we have to get rid of the fake stuff. Sometimes we don't know how to do this, especially if our feelings are strong ones. To protect ourselves we say, "You make me angry" or "I'm angry," and let it go at that, because to be angry is an acceptable feeling. People use anger as a cover-up for more vulnerable feelings. The goal is to understand what is hidden beneath the anger. That is where the real feelings live — feelings of hurt, embarrassment, guilt, fear, rejection, confusion, loneliness, being unappreciated, ignored; you can add whatever others you think of.

My friend Nicole told me a sad story: "My mother-in-law was an attractive woman," she said, "quite distinguished looking. Molly saw changes in her lifetime that were incredible. She went from the horse and buggy age to the jet plane.

"In her heart of hearts she would have liked to graduate from a prestigious college, such as Smith or Vassar. But she didn't, so she educated herself. She painted, took art lessons, made jewelry, went to the opera, and designed her own clothes. Everything Molly wore matched. She thought of herself as a 'classy lady.' She looked pretty, her house looked pretty, but her life wasn't pretty.

"Her mother died when she was young and left her to take care of many brothers and sisters. And after her husband died, she lived alone for many years, until she herself died at ninety-five."

Nicole paused a moment before going on.

"A woman who was doing a video tape of the elderly went to my mother-in-law's home a few years before she died, to ask Molly questions about her memories of her family and her personal relationships. Molly never kept things in, so she didn't mind talking, but this time she said something unkind about everyone — her late husband, her children, her friends. In fact, she didn't have a nice word to say about anybody and told the woman, 'I had to wait for everyone in my family to die before I could live my life.'

"Luckily, the woman never ran the video for the charity she works for. Instead," Nicole said, "she gave it to me and I buried it.

"It was all very painful, and the strange thing was, although she wasn't a loving or giving person, Molly was a terrific mother-in-law. She never demanded much. She didn't interfere, and she was incredibly independent. I think she liked me because I expected little from her, and the world knew her as a wonderful woman who kept a wonderful home.

"But she taught me a lesson. You can't just say 'Yes, yes!' and stuff your feelings inside. If you do, anger builds; so I try to make the relationships between me and my daughters-in-law *open* and loving."

Molly's story displays a profound lack of authenticity. Most of us don't live this kind of pretense. We can only speculate about the things going on in her head. She saw other people as needing from her because, when she was young, she had been giving all the time. Perhaps because she gave so much to her family, she harbored enormous resentment for years and years. Even as an elderly woman, she was carrying around the burden of raising all her siblings. History casts shadows on the present, and sometimes people get stuck, so from time to time it may be a good idea to ask yourself, if you had one more day to live, what would you say about your relationships?

Molly never asked for anything, so everyone read her as independent and capable. But sometimes it's *important* to ask for things we need. You can't be a doormat if you want people to love you. You have to speak up, instead of suffering silently and discounting your own wants. There has to be honesty in relationships, and we have to deal with issues that arise in an acceptable, well-thought-out way — to open up to our children and tell them how we feel.

I-messages are a way to do this that have less potential for causing arguments. An I-message is nonblaming and permits you to express yourself without putting another on the defensive. It allows you to take responsibility for your feelings. Such messages begin with the words *I feel* or *I think*. Here's an example:

"I feel [annoyed, irritated, upset] when you tell me ten minutes before twelve that you can't meet me for lunch."

Do *not* say, *"I feel that* **you** *are annoying* [irritating, etc.]." That's an accusation, not a statement of your own feelings. I-messages only work if they focus on what *you're* thinking or feeling.

Notice what happens when you say "I feel *that...*" By adding "that" to your statement, you avoid expressing your feeling. The sentence can only end with some reference to another person, an idea, or something outside yourself. Keep the focus on expressing *your feeling* at the time: anger, disappointment, sadness, frustration....

These messages don't point a finger at anyone. They are a way of opening yourself up to others and allowing them to know who you are. They give you a chance to explore the inner person — the real you. Even if you don't do anything more than to sort out your own values, the convictions you have about what is important in life, what is right and wrong or good and bad, you are far more likely to start to think clearly.

When you open yourself up, there are risks:

• The other person may tune out for various reasons. They may be overwhelmed by their own problems or they may not be of a giving nature.

• The other person may use your self-disclosure in a future disagreement.

• The other person may not take your feelings seriously.

But a mother-in-law has to take such risks if she wants a meaningful relationship with her in-law children. Moreover, she must be careful not to interject her feelings at an inappropriate moment. Timing is crucial — said William James, "The art of being wise is the art of knowing what to overlook."

We mothers-in-law recognize our irritation. There is tension in our bodies, but we have options. We can ask the question, is this really worth making an issue over? If we want a successful relationship, it's important to let some things go. Then we can relax our bodies so we don't take the irritation in. Instead, we can just breathe it out.

And just as knowing *what* to overlook is important, it's also crucial to know *when* to overlook. If you come to babysit for your daughter-in-law on a day when one child is sick, the dog is running loose, the place is a mess, and the baby is crying, this isn't the day to open yourself up and tell her how you feel about the way she manages her household. Furthermore, her household isn't your business. If you value a clean house and your daughter-in-law has a dirty one, it doesn't affect you. But if you absolutely feel you must say something, wait till things are calmer — and choose your words very carefully.

You could say, "When I'm babysitting and the house is in disarray, I worry because I feel afraid I won't be able to find what I need."

In any case, when you send an "I feel" message, you have to be prepared to deal with a reaction. There will always be one. The emotional temperature of the other person will go up. Then you must set aside your feelings for the moment. You have to not only acknowledge the other person's, but deal with them, too.

Many of us comment without listening. If you haven't the time to pay attention to the response, it's often better to take deep breaths and bite your tongue.

Daniel was at a party, seated at a table next to Hilda, his mother-in-law. He was growing a mustache and it was just growing in, so he scratched it. Hilda turned to him and said, "It itches, doesn't it, darling?"

"Yes! How do you know?"

She said, "I remember how it was when Lisl was born."

Hilda was not afraid of exposing herself — sharing a very private moment. She allows herself to be intimate with her son-in-law in a non-threatening way, and humor is the vehicle she uses to bridges the gap between generations.

Another time Daniel was busy in his office, having a difficult day, when the phone rang. Hilda said, "Daniel, How many days does September have?"

"Thirty, Mom. Don't you remember the poem, 'Thirty days hath September. . . .'".

She listened patiently, and when he got to the end, said, "Darling, I can't remember how many days there are in September, how do you expect me to remember a whole poem?"

As a listener, you have to read beyond the words. What Hilda is really saying is "I love you." She's exposing her vulnerability, too, and this is what makes her human.

Let's look again at the "birthday card incident" mentioned on page 124. When your daughter-in-law tells you that you missed her birthday, you could say, "Oh, I'm sorry you're upset. But I do want you to know I wish you a happy birthday." State your values. Explain why birthday cards are not important to *you*: "In our family we never had a tradition of sending cards. We always telephoned each other. Would that please you?"

And then you have to realize that birthday cards have to do with your daughter-in-law's value system, her ties to her family, what she learned growing up, her roots. She sees them as an expression of love. If she doesn't get one, there is great disappointment — a lot of stuff is churned up for her.

On the other hand, birthday cards are no big deal to you because your family didn't send them. Nevertheless, you have to hear your daughter-in-law and understand her attachments. You have to set aside your judgement and say, How important is this for me? What do I want to accomplish? We all have different value systems.

If you are really interested in building good feelings, then you need to put the other person's needs first. Be careful to respect what is important to her. As long as there is no cost to you, and no conflict with your values, it shouldn't be hard. Why not treat your daughter-in-law's needs as you would a best friend's, and give her pleasure?

Here is the birthday interaction again, this time in straight talk with an "I feel" message.

Mother-in-law: "I feel *terrible that I forgot to send you a birthday card, because you're like a daughter to me and I didn't mean to hurt you.*"

Now, this mother-in-law must wait for a response. What do you think it might be? How would you feel if someone said this to you?

The important thing to remember is, when you give a feeling message, do not defend yourself. Just *listen, clarify what you heard,* and *feed it back.*

If change is going to occur, it has to be because both mother-in-law and son or daughter-in-law want to please each other. You have to tell yourself, This is who my children are, and I want a good relationship, so I'll have to be the one to understand them.

Here's an example of a very simple interaction with an "I feel" message. Practice so you can get the hang of it. Then, try some yourself with friends. A mother-in-law visits her daughter-in-law and son in their new apartment.

Mother-in-law: "I feel *wonderful that you asked me to visit. You've done a lovely job decorating. Everything looks great — the new and the old. I think it must have been really hard with both of you working full time.*"

The message is to let your children understand how welcome you feel and what you think. Note indeed, how in this message, both are easily communicated. It will feel strange at first to speak this way, but if you persist, after a while it *will* feel natural. In the end the results will be rewarding.

Here is another interaction — less simple, but it presents no risk.

Sean visits his parents each year to celebrate Christmas. They live three states away from his mother-in-law, a widow, who feels lonely during the holiday season. She can ignore her feelings, put on a happy face and build resentment, or offer the following "I feel" message.

Mother-in-law Nancy: "I feel *sad and lonely every Christmas when you go away, because I would like to spend the holidays with you and my grandchildren.*"

By being straight, this mother-in-law lets her children know who she is and how she feels. The intent is to give her children feedback on how their behavior has impacted on her emotionally. She follows this up with a question.

Nancy : "*How do you feel about what I just said to you?*"

Sean: "*I hear you, but I never get to see my mother.*"

Nancy: "*It sounds like you're feeling annoyed at what I said. I hear your frustration. I understand that you want to spend time with your parents, but I still feel lonely.*"

Sean: "*Well, I don't know what we can do about it.*"

Nancy: *I understand this is your tradition. But it's hard for me to be alone.*"

This dialogue sequence doesn't get *resolved*; however, by putting her cards on the table, this mother-in-law still has had the opportunity to express her feelings. And there is a possibility she can get something. If Nancy and Sean work at problem solving, here are some of the solutions they might discuss:

- alternate the Christmas holiday between parents
- have an early or late celebration with mother-in-law
- have the children host Christmas and have both parents stay with them
- bring the mother-in-law to the son-in-law's parents
- have the mother-in-law visit a friend at children's expense.

You may come up with even other, and more creative, ideas.

Clearly, to be a successful mother-in-law, one who is close to her children, a parent has to reprogram expectations, become self-observant, and learn to communicate skillfully. You may at first feel these techniques are an artificial way of expressing yourself, and be tempted to give up. Don't. They can open the doorway to relationships, and allow you to achieve greater clarity of thought and speech.

Communication takes much concentration so that our ideas are heard the way we intended them to be heard, and not misconstrued. Your success will depend on using the skills often, until they become part of you.

When you begin to practice, give some thought to the issues you want to address. Know what you want to accomplish, and address *only* one issue at a time. Then plan ahead.

How will you address this issue? With whom? When? Where? Are there risks to saying what you have in mind? Maybe you want to think things over? If you're sure you are comfortable with what you are going to say, write it out. Writing will help to fix the words in your memory. Rehearse. Listen how the words sound. Practice in front of a mirror. Out loud. Calmly. Finally, test the issues on a friend. Role play the scene and watch how your friend reacts. If he or she is defensive, rehearse nondefensive responses such as:

- *"I understand what you're saying, even though I see it another way."*
- *"Sorry you feel that way. Tell me why."*
- *"We seem to have different points of view about this."*

Patience and Persistence Payoff

Your ability to communicate depends on preparation and practice. No one is one-hundred percent successful all the time. So relax. Don't be discouraged if you make mistakes. Disappointment comes when you're *too eager*. Be patient with yourself.

Although you may want to try working out situations right away, it's better not to attempt it if you are in a stressful situation. Wait for things to calm down and play for time by saying, "I have to think about this."

It's almost always better to say nothing than to endanger a relationship.

Pat yourself on the back for each small change you make. Say, "Good for me! I'm not where I was a few weeks ago."

If you mess up a second time, and you might, be kind to yourself again. Laugh it off. How many babies would learn to walk if they quit the third time they fell?

Communicating is basic to relationships, essential for establishing bonds, and critical in understanding people better. It will not always be smooth going, but there is no limit to what you can achieve. Nothing worth having comes about by sheer luck. "Man's happiness in life," writes Chinese philosopher Ch'en Tu-hsiu, "is the result of man's own effort and is neither the gift of God nor a spontaneous natural product."

Your son and daughter-in-law live nearby and you see them at least once a week. You've recently become quite concerned that your daughter-in-law seems withdrawn and cool toward you. You'd like to have a social, if not intimate, friendship with her. You take this action:

    a. You do nothing, waiting for her to reach out when she's ready.

    b. You ask your son to talk to her and try to fix things up.

    c. You say to your son, in her presence, "Maybe if your wife ever talks to me again..."

    d. You tell her that she's behaving childishly.

    e. You tell her, in a private conversation, that you value the relationship and you hope she can feel okay about talking with you when there's something wrong.

Are you building a foundation for solid communication here?

    a. This may be ok for a while — just be sure she knows you're ready to talk when she is.

    b. You're expecting your son to be the go-between. You're going to have to take the risk and ask her yourself.

    c. This sort of indirect aggression is not healthy for any of you.

    d. Direct rebuke won't make you any points either. Her behavior may or may not be childish, but you haven't yet earned your wings as her parent, so this is out of line.

    e. Now you're talking!

Chapter 7

FROM EXPECTATION
TO REALITY
*"This is not what I thought
it would be like"*

*I*n order to know other human beings (and clearly, we mothers-in-law want to know our children and their mates), we have to know first who we are — not the outside person in the mirror, but the human being within. Choosing to read this book suggests you have already begun to have thoughts about yourself. It is a beginning, not only toward changing relations with your in-law children, but toward working on the "unfinished you," by altering unexamined expectations from years past that influence your behavior.

By "unexamined expectations" I mean the assumptions about life that are passed down from one generation to the next without conscious awareness but continue to shape values long after their original purpose has vanished. These values are often signaled in speech with the words, "should" and "ought."

To understand the present generation, you have to see what happened in previous ones. Observe your married children and their spouses; see if they are weighed down with too many "shoulds" and "oughts." Next, see if you yourself are, then ask:
- What kind of home did I grow up in?
- Were my parents supportive and flexible or controlling and judgemental?

- Did they take care of my needs or neglect them?
- What were my parents' values?
- Did they express feelings or hide them?
- Were they committed to each other?
- Did they listen to what I had to say?
- Did I meet my parents' expectations?
- Do I expect my children to meet my expectations of them?

These questions, and others like them, will help you sort out the unexamined beliefs in your *own* mind, by allowing you to see what keeps you tied to the past.

To enhance your life and discover who you are, it helps to talk to a trusted friend, or perhaps a therapist, about the patterns you've learned while growing up. And honest, straight talk is what this book is all about. It's also about what pushes our buttons and why. About beliefs and expectations that cause members of a family to express animosity toward each other for years, beliefs that cause pain, beliefs that might be found wanting.

When you work at identifying habitual attitudes or actions you learn more about yourself — take for instance, building resentment and cashing in your angers. Do you typically say to yourself, "I can't stand it any more, I've had enough"?

Think about some of the assumptions you've held about your family that you may want to change, assumptions that create distance between children, in-law children, and grandchildren.

To maintain closeness, you must not only get rid of your inaccurate perceptions, but admit your flaws and change your ingrained, unproductive patterns to productive ones. If you've spent years thinking and acting certain ways, those old viewpoints are a part of you, and they tend to be repeated throughout your lifetime. You most likely believe them blindly as if they were fact.

For example these may include "acting nice" and "giving in to others," in other words, being overly compliant because you lack self-esteem. Of course, you tell yourself, such behavior is better than making waves. But there are tradeoffs. It causes you discomfort, and the relationship at hand suffers because it isn't honest.

Some mothers-in-law, on the other hand, make too many demands. Do you have the unexamined assumption that your children have to love and respect you just because you're older, and that any difference of opinion is *disrespectful*, that age alone gives you permission to be right and know everything better? Years ago, people were raised with this idea. Today, we mothers-in-law have to prove ourselves many times over as we age, because our society worships youth. What we say as an elder is no longer considered wisdom, as it was when people lived in a more structured society. In our computer age, change is what life is about. It's also about acquiring a generosity of spirit and learning to forgive yourself for your own stupidity. It's about getting rid of unrealistic expectations that you compulsively hold on to, expectations that build barriers to intimacy.

These may include beliefs that you feel are absolute. Inside, they seem like rock-bottom truths, but in fact, they are not. You believe them *because* you haven't examined them. Others may or may not see them as truths, but realistically the goals they espouse cannot be met, and lead to disappointment.

Very few lives can't stand improvement, and the more empty yours seems to be, the more you may try, inappropriately, to live through your children — assisting them, advising them, making demands on them. Instead, you really have to *let go*. What does this mean? Letting go means you understand that your children are not carbon copies of you. They have different ideas, values, opinions, likes, and dislikes. You have to learn to respect their healthy independence. Paradoxically, loosening the reins means a closer relationship, because the tighter you hold on to another person, the more resistance you get. To let go fosters autonomy — you become "real." It can increase self-understanding, and add a new perspective to your life, that allows you to take responsibility for, and invest in, yourself, for *your* own needs and growth.

What kind of memory of your relationship do you want your children to preserve, if not a legacy of love, caring, and concern for others? If this is your goal, it's time to work at it. In order to do so, you have to heal your *own* emotional wounds, to examine parts of *your* mind that were left untended at important stages in your development. To be able to understand others, consider childhood needs *you* had that were unmet. These will clue you in to better understand what may have led to all kinds of negative feelings — to fear, distrust, jealousy, confusion, and to controlling your world in order to protect yourself from pain.

Fortunately, a mother-in-law *can* assert her needs, without stepping on other members of her family. She can begin by working to understand herself, and to become sensitive to the needs of others as well.

How Well Do You Know Yourself?

Things in your life (as in mine) may not be working. Many of us find it easier to cast blame than admit this. We don't look at ourselves. We say, "I'm angry at my son/daughter-in-law," or "I feel put-upon by my children."

Most of us cannot look at our troubled relationships and say, "I'm wrong," and "I'm causing anger," or ask the question, "What's going on?"

We don't stop to think about what the other person is feeling, or recognize that we have faults — traits others dislike. The rationale is to keep blaming the other. In doing so we feel justified and self-righteous. But nothing is resolved unless we look inward to our own unexamined behavior, because, and this bears repeating — *you cannot change another, you can only change yourself.*

It takes courage to accept that there is a best of us and a worst of us, that within we have wisdom and understanding, that, at times, all of us act foolishly, even intolerantly, yet every heart embodies elements of despair and incorporates hope. We are a mixture of all things. I believe that, if I can handle changing patterns and make adjustments, you can, too. All you need is determination — a willingness to let your old life end and a new one begin.

So take the next step. Ask yourself questions when things don't go right. To find out who you really are, respond honestly. Say, "What am *I* doing?" and "*How* can *I* change?" You may benefit by taking a chance and asking another person what you are not doing right. It is important to know up front, you probably won't like what you will hear. But the feedback will be thought-provoking.

Also, ask yourself, "How much effort am I willing to make?" Becoming self-aware means putting up with a certain amount of anxiety, as you did when you gave your infant that scary first bath. Although you are already in an uncomfortable situation, the old discomfort is familiar. For a while, you have to trade familiar discomfort for new discomfort. A major step toward becoming a bigger, more spontaneous person is to allow yourself to look at things differently — therefore, you must examine your unexamined beliefs.

Self-awareness takes a lot of time and effort. It is a complicated business and most of us are too impatient and protective of ourselves to invest that time, so we remain stuck. But difficult as it may be to adopt new beliefs and other ways of thinking, to relinquish control, to move forward and let your adult children be who they are, it will be worthwhile in the long run. If you have a willingness to leave the irresistibly familiar, then you *can let go*. To have healthy relationships and become a successful mother-in-law, you have to get "unstuck."

When you first feel something, what you feel, generally, is previous hurts, but when you wait, you can figure out what is old and what is new, and often see alternative solutions to problems. When you want to move toward better relationships, you have to be open to learning what you need to know. Hear information without getting angry. Otherwise you will jump to conclusions and not dig out the truths you need to free yourself or at least to modify your inappropriate behaviors. And it *will* be worthwhile to tolerate your turmoil, to look at your discontentment, to get past your helplessness. In fact, "The life which is unexamined," wrote Plato, "is not worth living."

What "Should" Mother-In-Lawing Be Like, Anyway?

The "shoulds" and "oughts" in our head are a direct out-growth of unexamined beliefs. When we feel insecure they protect us and validate our parents' rules which we've internalized. We all hold some of our parents' expectations. No one is totally free of them, it's just a matter of degree. They are child-oriented explanations that were true when we were young, and if unfulfilled, they cause people to feel unloved. Maybe yours include some of the following:

• My married children should show me respect because I'm their parent.

• My married children should know what I need even without being told.

• My married children should not make decisions without first consulting me, because Mother knows best.

• It's my son/daughter-in-law's responsibility to make sure my child and I have a close relationship.

• My daughter/son-in-law should dress the way I like to see her/him look.

• I'm always available for my married children; even if I have to cancel vacation plans, meetings, etc., it's all right.

• My child can do no wrong. It's the fault of the spouse.

• My son/daughter-in-law should love me because of the wonderful person I gave him/her — a spouse who is able to earn a great living, raise children, run a household, etc.

• My son/daughter-in-law should spend money on the children, not on entertainment or vacations.

• My married children should take care of me. They owe me.

• My daughter/son in law should appreciate my humor... quirks... enthusiasms as my children do.

• A working mother should relieve her children by babysitting the grandchildren on weekends.

When you study these unexamined expectations, you will see they can be guilt-producing and self-defeating as well as unrealistic. Most are unattainable, certainly not automatic. That fact may cause you pain, but they all breed confusion and anger. Insisting on them will prevent you from pursuing your dream of a loving relationship with your married children.

In the best of all possible worlds, if we could have our own way, of course we'd see *our* expectations fulfilled. They lead to our comfort and security. But we can't and don't have it our way all the time. It's not crazy to want to be comfortable. As human beings we have a natural yearning to want things to go the way we like. But we have to make modifications in our behavior. And you get something for giving up your erroneous expectations. *You get more of what you want.*

Becoming Realistic

To understand how to change unexamined expectations, take a look at the realistic replacements in the following examples:

• My married children should show me respect, because I'm their parent.

The Realistic Replacement: Married children will respect or not respect you because of your actions.

• Married children should know what I need even when I don't tell them.

The Realistic Replacement: My children are not mind readers. If I don't tell them what I want, they will not know.

• Married children should not make decisions without first consulting me because Mother knows best.

The Realistic Replacement: Adult children have to make their own decisions, live with the consequences, and learn from them.

• It's my daughter/son-in-law's responsibility to make sure my child and I have a close relationship.

The Realistic Replacement: The nature of my relationships remains solely with me. It would be nice if we were friends but I cannot control her/his emotional responses.

• My daughter/son-in-law should dress the way I like to him/her to look.

The Realistic Replacement: My in-law children — like my own children — are individuals. They have the right to their own taste.

• I'm always available for my married children; even if I have to cancel vacation plans, meetings, etc.

The Realistic Replacement: I have a life of my own. It's appropriate to put my needs first as they are as valid as my children's and grandchildren's. In an emergency, I'll drop everything and help them.

• My child can do no wrong. Any problems are the fault of the spouse.

The Realistic Replacement: My child has virtues as well as faults. Sometimes he's right, and sometimes he's wrong. That's the nature of being human.

• My daughter/son-in-law should love me because of the wonderful mate I gave her/him — educated and able to earn a great living, raise children, run a household...

The Realistic Replacement: Love takes time to build. She/he will love me because of my behavior toward her/him.

• Because I am older, my needs should come first.

The Realistic Replacement: There is more than one criterion for determining who comes first. Age may be a factor — young or old — but sometimes other needs come first.

• My married children should take care of me. Look what I did for them.

The Realistic Replacement: It would be nice if I could count on them to always be there for me, but they have other responsibilities. I have to find different resources for my emotional, financial, and physical well being.

• My daughter/son-in-law should appreciate my humor... quirks... enthusiasms as my children do.

The Realistic Replacement: My in-law children may not appreciate my humor... quirks... and enthusiasms, but I have to be open minded and accept them and their differences.

• A working mother-in-law should relieve her children by taking the grandchildren on the weekends.

The Realistic Replacement: A working woman has to be realistic and set limits. She tells herself, I cannot give to my children the way a nonworking mother-in-law can, because my job leaves me exhausted.

Study both the unexamined expectations and the realistic replacements. You will notice that the unexamined expectations are stricter — more judgmental. They are full of "shoulds" that can easily lead to bad feelings. They are as limiting as a one-lane highway, because there is no room for maneuvering.

The realistic replacements, by contrast, are benevolent, less harsh; they permit movement. They allow you to give more to yourself, even though there are losses. If you care about your children and your grandchildren — and of course you do — you'll be one of the wise women who will start on a process of change and work toward becoming a successful mother-in-law. There are a whole range of procedures available to you. You might find one or more of the five steps described below helpful.

Changing Unexamined Expectations

Step One: Examine Your Unexamined Expectations: Choose two or three beliefs from the previous list that feel true for you, or add your own to work with. Pick the ones that are gut issues, that trigger something inside. Take out a piece of paper and jot them down. Then ask yourself the following questions:

• Does this belief affect my relationship with my in-law children or with others who are important to me?

• Does this belief make me feel negative emotions often?

What feelings are they? Anger? Fear? Jealousy? Others not mentioned? (If you can't think of an emotion, do you notice a physical response? Try to get in touch with how your body feels: tense? headachy? tired? Are your hands cold or sweaty? Is your stomach in knots? These are all clues.)

• Is my speech filled with "You *never*" or "You *always*"?

(When we expect our children or in-law children to *always* treat us lovingly or as a revered elder, we will be disappointed and create problems for ourselves because they can't *always* do that. Life is a series of problems to be solved. Now that you've found some to work on, let's see how it is done.)

Step Two: Make Conscious Changes:

• Make a chart with two columns — "faulty expectations" on the left side, and "realistic and attainable replacements" on the right. Jot down all your interactions. At the end of each day examine them. Did you operate out of the realistic belief system? Then check the right side of your chart. Now look at the unexamined beliefs you checked. What would you like to change?

• Instead of automatically repeating an old habit, slow down. Give yourself time to reflect. Identify what you feel and ask yourself why do I feel this way? What triggered these feelings? Think objectively, and jot everything down. Soon you will see certain feelings keep reoccurring. These are patterns and they trigger negative behavior. Consider asking yourself, "What benefits am I receiving from acting this way?" "How can I change these interactions?"

• Be prepared to feel uneasy for a while — this is not a comfortable process. You will feel less spontaneous because you are constantly thinking, processing each situation before acting.

Because you are responding in new ways your emotional reactions will be different. You may not notice any differences in yourself, but your friends will tell you, "You're not the same."

Step Three: Follow These Helpful Hints:
• Keep the Expectations Chart next to your bed.
• Read it each morning and evening.
• In order to remind yourself to think and act differently, wear your watch backwards. This will jolt you, help interrupt old thought patterns.
• Change the focus and concentrate on the concerns of the moment.
• When you talk on the telephone, place an index card in front of you that says, in bright print — *Realistic Beliefs Only!*.
• When feeling physically agitated, take a few deep breaths, count to ten, and call a friend.
• Write a letter and get your feelings out, but don't mail the letter.
• Go for a brisk walk on your lunch break, or meditate.

Step Four: Evaluate your Interactions
• Look at the consequences of your interactions.
• What did you say, do, and feel?
• What did your in-law child do and say?
• What did you observe?
• What responses were you aiming for?
• Were your goals met?
• What feedback did you receive from others?
• Were you acting from unexamined beliefs or realistic beliefs?

Step Five: Stick With It
• In any conversation, when both sides have strong feelings, do the following:
     - Change the topic. Later, you may be able to reconcile differences amiably.

- Do some imaging. See a bouquet of flowers, picture your grandchild singing "White Christmas."

- Remember, change is *gradual*. It comes in increments. If you make a mistake, it's not the end of the world. On the other hand, when things go well, acknowledge the positive steps you've made. Reward yourself — take a bubble bath, collect points toward a new outfit, buy yourself a plant, book, tapes, or eat dinner out.

These are just a few suggestions. They aren't the only guidelines to follow. You may have other ideas about how to change your unexamined expectations. What is important is to get started.

Like a healthy reducing plan, change is slow. It's a four letter word: *WORK*. And you won't move ahead by making promises to start Monday or next week.

Of course it's tempting to say, "The old way was fine for my parents, and if it was right for them, it's right for me," or "I can't change now," and give up. But then you close the door to a better self. Tell yourself the past was the past, that it's time to live in the present.

The Yiddish word *mensch* is hard to translate, because it has many overtones, but when someone calls you a *mensch*, it is a great compliment. It means you are a decent human being, that your behavior exemplifies the best in a person. And when you act in a *menschlich* fashion this means you act in an honorable, understanding, kind, caring, and thoughtful way, a way that elicits respect, a way we all aspire to be with our children. If you don't work at becoming a decent human being, there is the possibility that, when you least expect it, your children will pay you back with the resentment they have stored. And the payback will be in whatever currency they have. There is always the chance that you may be frozen out of their lives and the lives of your grandchildren, too.

When a mother-in-law changes direction, it's a truism that her children will follow. When you move toward wisdom and inner peace, others move with you. The first thing you need to do is to gain a better perspective.

Gaining New Perspective

Let's look at two mothers-in-law dealing with similar situations.

The first, because her son doesn't visit weekly now that he is married, acts out, saying in a healthy voice, "If I had died, you'd know about it when you hear from the funeral parlor."

She erroneously interprets her son's infrequent visits as rejection, and feels this as a diminishment of his love. She doesn't realize she has now become a queen mother instead of a queen. Through her upbringing, she has acquired the belief that a child is supposed to honor its mother — meaning do whatever she wants — when in truth a parent has to earn that honor, and a person is supposed to cleave unto his/her mate.

The second mother-in-law says, "I don't have to worry about my child anymore. I'm glad he found someone to love and be loved. I don't need to be the most important person in his life. What I want now is to be the most important person in *my* life."

Here, you can see that in similar circumstances, and because of perspective, one mother-in-law finds fault, the other a blessing in her child's marriage. To love is to give, to grow. As conditions change, we mothers-in-law have to change, too. We need to understand our actions — what they mean and how they are interpreted by others.

Your feelings are God-given and natural, and you don't have to be ashamed of them. A person can't help having feelings about almost everything, and when something is important your emotions become more intense. But they're not unchangeable! As with all things in life, you have choices you can make and things you can do with your emotions.

First, you have to recognize them, experience them, and evaluate what you are feeling. You have to open your mind to hear what is going on inside you. This is just the beginning, because, after you hear and know what you feel, you need to think about a course of action.

When we act mindlessly, manipulatively, or melodramatically, we encounter hurt and mistrust. We have to set limits on ourselves, understand that our way is not the only way. The best approach is to accept that there is more than one point of view, that ideas don't necessarily resonate the same for any two human beings. It is possible for more than one individual to be right because each has a different perspective, just as there are many approaches to the same town. Anyone who comes from another direction is driving on a right road, too.

I believe the average mother-in-law, like the average daughter- or son-in-law, wants to journey toward love. Then why are in-law stories crammed full of emotional bruises, instead of the natural give-and-take that friends know? Our heads recognize it oughtn't to be like this, but our unexamined beliefs get in the way. This is especially true when it comes to gift giving, as we'll see in the following chapter.

They've done it again. Your daughter and son-in-law have joined a local group working to have certain "offensive" books removed from the local library. They express concern for exposure of their children — your grandchildren — to "obscenity and profanity." You are a strong believer in First Amendment freedom and object vehemently to any notion of censorship. You say:

    a. "Why didn't you talk with me first? You know how hard I've worked to support the library"

    b. "I'm embarrassed that you would take such an ignorant position."

    c. "You have a right to your opinions, but you should know better than this."

    d. "It's okay, whatever you think..."

    e. "Can you tell me how you arrived at this viewpoint?"

    f. "Who talked you into this?"

And how do your responses stack up to the realistic approaches you learned about in this chapter?

    a. "My children are not mind readers. If I don't tell them how I feel, they will not know."

    b. "Adult children have to make their own decisions, live with the consequences, and learn from them."

    c. "My in-law children — like my own children — are individuals. They have the right to their own taste."

    d. "Are you really that accepting of 'whatever you think'? Aren't your feelings valid, too?"

    e. Nice work! "The best approach is to accept that there is more than one point of view, that ideas don't necessarily resonate the same for any two human beings."

    f. "Instead of automatically thinking your children are being led, slow down so you don't say something you'll regret."

Chapter 8

FROM THE BOTTOM
OF YOUR HEART...
Gift-Giving for the Other Mother

Paul knew his mother would be pleased. He was taking her to lunch at one of those hot-ticket bistros — the kind that require reservations weeks in advance. He planned to tell her about the great promotion he'd just received at the plant. To frost the cake, he was wearing one of the new shirts — he'd decided on the red one — that she gave him for his birthday.

As soon as they were seated at a comfortable window table, Paul beamed, "I sure like this shirt, Ma." She didn't bat an eye: "So, what's wrong with the blue one?"

The story has been told a thousand times, but the point remains: It's really tough to please some people. And gifts are one of the most obvious ways that truth rears its ugly head.

Can You Believe It?

Gifts — even those that are selected thoughtfully with the receiver in mind — represent what the giver believes is important. Each of us thinks that what *we* believe is right — the truth — and truth for each of us reflects our experience. But there are no objective truths. What is wonderful to one person is not necessarily wonderful for someone else.

Members of the same family generally mirror each other and have similar values. But in-law children come from other families, and don't necessarily share the same beliefs and assumptions. They don't know our beliefs about gifts, and we don't know theirs. If we tune in to each other, we can gain important insights to understanding our respective attitudes about giving and receiving.

Speaking of Gifts...

There were both mothers-in-law and daughters-in-law in my homespun survey who responded with the following:

"My mother-in-law gave me a gift whenever my children had a birthday. She said, 'You're the one who gave me this wonderful grandchild. You're the one who deserves a gift.' "

"My mother-in-law would always bring us something from her trips, which said she thought about us. It made me feel loved and cherished."

"My daughter-in-law takes the time to buy something I would like. I might be shopping with her and mention something is pretty, and when holiday time comes, it's there for me."

"My mother-in-law is extremely generous. She hardly ever comes to visit without a gift. They are given with love, and I appreciate her efforts. She has good taste, but every once in a while she brings a clinker. I don't want to tell her to bring it back, because it would hurt her."

"I have two daughters-in-law. One doesn't always have a knack for finding the right thing, but when I told her a gift was something I couldn't use, I received gifts that weren't personal. My other daughter-in-law always seems to find appropriate gifts. She puts a lot of thought into pleasing me, but I always tell *both* how much I appreciate their gifts."

"One Sunday, my mother-in-law showed up on our doorstep with a beautifully wrapped package. She didn't say anything when she put the package down except, 'I hope you like it.'

It was our wedding anniversary, and my husband and I had completely forgotten, because at that time the fourth child had just come home from the hospital. (The other kids were three, five, and seven.) I wondered what the gift was for — someone's birthday? a holiday? — and then I realized it was our anniversary.

"Life was so involved then it'd just skipped by. But my mother-in-law never forgot a birthday or anniversary. The children could always depend on a present. She never even missed a card. She is so interested in the children; they are her whole life. When video cameras first came out, she took hours of them waving. My children love going to Grandma's, because she makes such a fuss over them, till this day she's interested in every detail of their lives.

"She tells the children their history and has made picture albums for every one. She isn't a 'perfect' mother-in-law, but who is? She *is* a wonderful grandmother, and it overcomes her shortcomings. I feel my children are so lucky to have so much time with someone who really cares about them. She gives them the right words along with her presence and presents."

These people seemed to be tuned in to each other and sensitive to each other's desires, even in the case where the daughter-in-law had to exchange a gift. The fact is that she was able to change directions after receiving feedback. To modify her own needs says this daughter-in-law was thinking about her mother-in-law's pleasure. There seems to be an openness in the relationship. The focus is not on the self. Each of the individuals seem to be thinking in terms of *family* — "us" rather than "me".

In giving, the mother or daughter-in-law is thinking about who the other is and what would feel good to her. When there are children, the youngsters feel the sincerity of the grandmother's affection and love. When she dropped off her gift, she let the pleasure be in the giving, and when we do this we nourish ourselves. Giving of self in a free way has its rewards — what we give comes back to us. All seem to appreciate the effort and the thoughtfulness of the other family member even more than the gift itself.

Lead Balloons and Lumps of Coal

Gift giving, alas, is not always a happy occasion. The act of giving or receiving a gift can trigger both happy and unhappy feelings. No matter what your age, gifts may be tied in to memories of not-so-merry Christmases past, to birthdays when you didn't receive what you had hoped for — when your sister got what you wanted. You may feel the old hurts and walk around with a critical-parent message in your head:

- "You're too clumsy for that."
- "It's too expensive."
- "You can't have that."
- "What did you expect? We're not *millionaires*."

You're an adult now, but you may still be behaving as if you were in a time warp, hearing your parents' words. Those old belief systems need to be repaired. It's time to sort out your own needs, and — just maybe — to try something new when it comes to giving and getting gifts.

Gifts, for some, can be a symbol of self-worth. A pricey sweater or piece of jewelry can be taken as a symbol that one is worth a lot; an inexpensive hand-made item, though fashioned with love, may produce bad feelings. The receiver who values gifts — and herself — in this way causes everybody to lose. In this person's faulty belief system, inexpensive gifts are considered an insult, and she chalks up another mark against the giver. Sad to say, it's not likely that such an individual will ever be able to get all her needs met.

Some People are Never Satisfied

One daughter-in-law told me, "I go crazy. Whenever I give a gift to my mother-in-law, she says, 'Thank you so much, but I don't need it. Could you return this?'"

My own mother used to say, "A pocketbook! I don't need a pocketbook. I need a nightgown (sweater, robe...) this year."

If you think that these responses were rude, you're quite right. These women lacked tact and sensitivity. Their upbringing left them without the social grace of how to accept a gift. You don't have to *like* a gift, but it's kind to let the giver know you appreciate the *thought*.

Perhaps these individuals didn't feel worthy of the gifts given. Trying to please them is difficult, at best. Whatever present they receive is inadequate — "wrong" is their constant motif. They are trying to enhance their self-image by what they think would be appropriate for you to give them, because they have to be in control.

There may be a void in each of these women that cannot be filled, an emptiness that perhaps goes back to childhood. They are too wounded to say, "Thank you. I appreciate your thought and efforts." They haven't learned that a gift is a tangible way to say, "You mean something special to me."

Mothers and children like the previous ones have to understand that gifts are an issue for them. They have to acknowledge the emptiness within, and fill it *themselves*. They cannot expect anyone else to. What they are otherwise saying, in effect, is "You cannot make me happy, no matter what you do, because I'm worthless."

The trouble is, of course, that such a response denies joy to the giver as well.

I wish for you the ability to receive a gift as the wonderful gesture it is, because, if you keep rejecting your childrens' efforts, they will cease. Your child will say, "Why should I bother? She won't ever think it's right."

Ultimately, we come back to the fundamental question: What kind of relationship do you want to have with your children and their spouses? Do you want to prove you are right, that the other is wrong, to raise barriers and set yourself up for disappointment? Or are you looking to show your children and in-law children that you love them? Life is a two way street; you usually get back what you put in.

"How Do I Reject Thee? Let Me Count the Ways..."

Any number of things may make the receiver of a gift uncomfortable, since gifts carry symbolic significance greater than their material value. Before you give your next gift, consider some other faulty beliefs that add to the complexity of gift giving:

• Some feel accepting gifts puts an individual in a one-down position.

• Some feel receiving a gift means they owe something.

• For some, gifts ignite competitive feelings.

• To *reject* a gift makes some people feel one-up.

• With money gifts (which are bottom-line countable), the receiver may measure only the dollar amount.

• Some givers see money as a right choice because they are not sensitive to what others like.

• Some gift receivers see a money gift as evidence the giver didn't care enough to make an effort to please.

Receiving a gift is an opportunity to take in pleasure and love. If you really want another person's love, you'd best not reject their material expressions of it.

Many (Un)Happy Returns

Sometimes, of course, a gift just doesn't fit — on your body or in your life. If we return the gifts our children give us, however, they may be disappointed or feel unappreciated. Some of us are fussier than others, but if you make a habit of returning gifts or never using or wearing them, it can hurt. It chips away at the giver's self-esteem.

Some in-law mothers and children have a special talent for knowing what gives the other pleasure, but most of us don't have that particular gift. You'll avoid a lot of disappointment if you don't assume that the other person "should have known..."

I believe it's helpful, in the interest of your long-term relationship with a son- or daughter-in-law, to talk openly about gifts. Tell each other what you like, or if perhaps you really *don't* need anything, tell them you would rather have a donation made to charity.

"You Shouldn't Have... Really!"

Any gift compliments, no matter what. But think how difficult a time many people have in *accepting* compliments. I remember my mother-in-law would accept a gift I spent days picking out with, "You shouldn't have bothered spending the money. You could have bought something nice for yourself," then put the gift in a drawer and never use it.

Alas, as she grew up she hadn't been taught to accept compliments well. Those who weren't taught to receive compliments gracefully usually reject them, feeling unworthy. On the other hand, she'd very generously hand me a few hundred dollars when our family would go on our summer vacation. "Go out," she'd say, "Have a night on the town on us" — and she wouldn't take no for an answer. It always interested me to watch how she could give but not receive.

Mother Strauss couldn't be given to because it tapped into her sense of powerlessness. Many of us are reluctant to accept a favor because it takes away our independence, and perhaps suggests that we are unable to take care of ourselves, even if only momentarily.

How many times have you heard, "My, that's a lovely blouse," and replied "This old thing?" Too many of us were brought up with few compliments. Taught not to get a "swelled head," we learned not to take in any of "the good stuff," to be critical, especially of ourselves.

Similarly, some mothers and sons and daughters-in-law equate the gift with the giver. But the gift and the giver are not one. You don't necessarily have to like the gift, but when a person goes out of his or her way to do something nice, I urge you to let the giver know you appreciate the thought and the effort. A simple "thank you" takes only a moment, and offers a welcome affirmation that the giver has done the right thing.

Are Giving and Receiving "Women's Work"?

Where is the law that says women must be responsible for all the gifts, telephone calls, greeting cards, and thank-you notes? Or that a daughter, as soon as she becomes a daughter-in-law, has to assume that job on behalf of her husband? If her husband grew up in a home where his mother took care of these responsibilities, he may expect his wife to do the same. And the cycle continues.

In the past, of course, such activities *were* a woman's domain. Most women had the time to handle these niceties because they didn't work outside the home. What's more, many *enjoyed* making the calls and shopping for the gifts.

Today, many women are the primary wage earners, and their only exclusive domains are childbearing and breast feeding. Everything else is negotiable, and Alex and his mate must address who has the inclination and the time to handle these jobs. The decision is theirs to make; it really doesn't matter, as long as the choice isn't fraught with resentment.

But we mothers-in-law must be careful of our own expectations here. Is it fair for us to hold our in-law children responsible for our own child's oversights? If mother is truly open-minded and willing to face her own blind spots, she will put the burden of responsibility where it belongs. If her son forgets her birthday, for example, she'll avoid blaming his wife: "Alex is responsible. My own child is the neglectful one." What's more, she'll recognize that forgetting a gift is usually an oversight, an act of *carelessness*, not evidence of a lack of *love*.

Traditions, Obligations, and Changing Times

Gift-giving traditions and the expectations surrounding them have changed a great deal in the past few decades. For my generation, the procedure was well defined: gifts for family members may have come from the heart, but they were clearly an obligation as well; for close friends only slightly less so. The tradition applied — with variations — to birthdays, weddings, birth of a child, anniversaries, Christmas and Hanukkah, bar and bat mitzvahs, christenings and other family holidays and traditions. Written thank-you notes, within a week or two following receipt of the gift, were also an obligation. Children were familiarized with these responsibilities early on, and began to handle them independently by the time they finished elementary school.

No more. Today's youngsters are growing up in a much more informal world. A phone call or face-to-face thank you is generally acceptable now. Overlooking a celebratory gift is no longer a capital crime. Times change. Thoughtful mothers-in-law will attempt to teach by example the traditions they consider important, but they won't expect their children and grandchildren to abide by them religiously.

But obligations are a double-edged sword. Often, instead of pleasure and a warming of our inner core, the experience of gift giving becomes another chore, another item on the shopping list. You've heard people say, "Oh, I *have* to buy him/her a gift." Gifts that come with a "have to" don't always create joy or intimacy. It's when you sincerely *want* to give a gift that it gives you as well as the receiver pleasure. It doesn't have to be a special occasion gift. It can merely be something you know the other would enjoy — a bit of serendipity, a newspaper clipping, a book, a tape, even a phone call. The thing that matters is the delight the object brings to the other. You know what I mean, because when it happens to you, you feel cared about.

The Art of "Self-Defense"

Throughout our lifetimes we adopt certain defense mechanisms to shield our unexamined beliefs. We use them when we deal with problems that cause us to feel emotional pain, preferring not to look at the negative parts of our personality. At the same time, however, they can be a way of fooling ourselves. Although every person employs an armload of defense mechanisms during a lifetime, most of us have a favored style. Common forms include *denial, projection,* and *overcompensation.* Here's how these work in the area of gift giving.

Projection. Amanda, who has recently married into a wealthy family, has a loving, generous mother-in-law, Nora. Because Amanda is totally accepted by the older woman, Nora showers her with elaborate gifts. Amanda is used to receiving simple presents from her own parents — and only when she's done something special for them — so she *projects* negative intent onto her in-law's gifts, attributing her *own* feelings to her mother-in-law to avoid taking responsibility for her deficiencies. Since Amanda doesn't feel comfortable accepting anything costly and doesn't acknowledge her feelings of inferiority, projection allows her *not* to see her mother-in law for the woman she is.

This helps Amanda maintain her belief system. It also keeps her from exploring her own feelings. She tells herself, "She's trying to win me over" or "There must be a reason she's buying me this."

If this daughter-in-law keeps building resentment and doesn't connect into her own feelings — most likely, old ways of thinking borrowed from her parents — she will eventually push Nora away.

Now let's turn to Brian and Wendy, who have a similar situation.

Wendy: "Mom and Dad are so nice. They bought us the sofa for Christmas. The one we love."

Brian: "I don't want their sofa."

Wendy: "It's a present!"

Brian: "It costs a fortune. I don't want it!"

Wendy: "Are you crazy? We love it!"

Brian: "When we can buy it, then we'll have it. Your parents are always trying to show me up. They never thought I was good enough for your ritzy family."

Again, we see negative intent projected onto in-laws. Brian does this to maintain his belief system — to avoid looking at his own insecurities, just as Amanda does.

But there is another factor operating here: Traditionally, the man is the provider and protector of his family, so Brian feels even more diminished when his in-laws buy what he considers an extravagant gift, even though the intention was totally benevolent. He feels they're infringing on his sphere of influence, and this causes resentment.

If there is money on one side of the family and not on the other, gift giving can become a big issue in a marriage. Brian and Amanda both have insecurities that color everything. Brian may be feeling inadequate, embarrassed, indebted, or that he will forever have to pay back.

In order to change his perspective and get to resolution, the couple have to share their feelings. If Brian can talk without denying his, and Wendy can just listen without saying, "You shouldn't feel that way," this young man might get past his anger and deal with the real issue. But Brian would need to know that his wife understood. Only then could he move to a position of comfort and accept the sofa. Then this young couple would have to decide how to handle issues like this in the future.

Take a few moments and ask yourself some practical questions:

- How do I *respond* to gifts?
- Do I see gifts in a negative or positive light?
- What makes me see them this way?

Denial. Denial is a way of *not letting ourselves know what we think.* We banish unacceptable points of view that we hold and pretend that we don't have them because they are unpleasant to acknowledge. Or we act them out without realizing it. We do this because, when we were young, we weren't *allowed* certain feelings, such as anger.

Consider this script: You feel your son made a poor choice in the selection of a mate. Your value system (which contains discriminating feelings against overweight people) says your daughter-in-law should be slender. But your son loves her the way she is, Rubensesque figure and all. When the young woman's birthday arrives, you buy your daughter-in-law an inappropriate gift, not conscious of what you are doing. Because you've struggled all your life to maintain a thin figure, your present to her is a year's subscription to a health club.

The denial — which veils criticism — is, you don't want to face the fact that she's not okay the way she is. The message is, *You aren't right for my son the way you are.* The gift is your way of saying, *I know how you should look.* It's hurtful, and it is more for this mother-in-law's self-esteem than for her daughter-in-law's pleasure.

This mother-in-law has buried her feelings to the point of nonrecognition. She is blind to the fact that she has blocked them out. If a friend brought up what she is doing, she would say, "Who, me?"

The denial occurs because she is not taking responsibility for her feelings when she clearly has them. If she did admit to them, she would have to struggle with the feeling of embarrassment. The situation won't ring any bells for her. Neither will she understand the pain her daughter-in-law will feel when she receives the gift. It may cause a rift between the two, especially if the daughter-in-law has been struggling with a weight problem, too. She might see the subscription to a health club as her mother-in-law's disapproval and misguided attempt to control her life. The hurt she feels may then be translated into anger, which can escalate into a no-win, no-relationship situation.

Denial teaches us that, if we don't acknowledge our feelings, we are not in charge of them. We behave without knowing why we are doing something, and don't realize the impact it has on another. If we could find the feelings we don't approve of and accept them, we would not act out.

In almost all families, certain ways of feeling were unacceptable. Think about your family of origin. Was denial one of the defense mechanisms you learned as a child in order to prevent punishment? (It was one *I* was well schooled in! "Don't cry, or you'll get something to cry about!" haunts me even today, having taught me to deny my feelings of hurt.)

By refusing to acknowledge what you do, you lose the opportunity to control your own destiny, and become alienated from inner forces. Whereas, if you are better able to understand your behavior, you make healthier judgements about when, and even if, to express yourself. Then you control your destiny.

Overcompensation. A third defense mechanism is *overcompensation*. The mother-in-law who overcompensates says every gift she receives is wonderful, lovely, terrific, marvelous — because *she can't take in the negative*.

If her in-law child gives her a stainless steel sculpture and her home is very traditional, decorated primarily in antiques, this mother-in-law will subvert her true feelings and say, "I love it. It's exactly what I wanted," and rave on and on, overcompensating for the fact that she doesn't care for the gift but has a desperate need to be liked. She's afraid of risking the other's disfavor. Although there is cover up with pretense, honesty would be better, because usually some of the real feelings manage to leak through. By facing what we do in a situation, we grow. If we don't, we hide truths from ourselves, and allow unconscious ways of acting to thwart us in our search for intimate relationships; hence, we must move beyond.

Gift-Giving Checklist

To make an objective assessment when it comes to gift giving, the first step is to be aware of what you are doing. Awareness gives you a choice over your behavior. Try to keep an open mind when you look at the following list. It will enable you to really see the message you are sending your children, along with the gifts you are giving.

• Whose needs do you want to satisfy, yours or the recipient's?

• Are you using gift giving as a means of competing with the other set of parents?

• Have you thought about how you distribute gifts to your grown children? Is it done haphazardly, or with concern for equitable distribution, or is the gift giving on the basis of need?

• Do you use gifts to keep the relationship going?

• How well do you know your in-law child's family of origin? What interpretations will they make of a gift, based on their background? For example, there are people who feel that flowers are a waste of money.

• Is this gift within your budget? Have you thought about how your in-law child will feel if the gift is a sacrifice for you? How would you feel if you received an expensive gift from someone you felt couldn't afford it?

• When you buy a gift, do you have the other person's interest at heart or are there other motivational factors at stake?

• Is this gift a repayment — tit-for-tat?

• Do you use a gift as a substitute for reforming? Is it permission to act inappropriately again — for example, screaming at in-law children, then buying them an expensive gift to compensate for guilt?

• Will the other person appreciate the gift?

What did *you* discover from examining this list? The quicker you have a clear sense of what you are doing, the sooner you can reshape your behavior. It may involve a struggle and lots of thinking, but you can do it.

On Gift Giving and Relationship Building

The most sensible standard, when giving a gift, is to try to pick out something the recipient would like to own. Easier said than done, isn't it? You can't always put yourself in the other's place. (When it comes to my in-law children, I find it very difficult for the results to match my best intentions. Try as I will to give a gift I think they would like, I'm not always right. Mothers-in-law are not psychic; we often don't guess correctly.)

To be really adept at gift giving requires one to be very attentive — to listen well, to really concentrate, to hear what is important to the other, to suspend one's own judgement. Sometimes even to read between the lines.

When you send the right messages, about gifts or anything else, your in-law children will be able to see you as a friend, someone to be close to, someone who exchanges signals that mean "I'm here for you," someone who'll listen when called, someone who helps the other feel alive when the weight of the world is pressing down.

One of the most important messages you can send to your children, and one of the most valuable gifts you can give them, is *respect*. Respect for their individuality, and for their status as independent adults.

Respect doesn't necessarily come with marriage, or parenthood, or age; it takes time to develop. Likewise, true friendship with an in-law child and his or her family can take years to build. If you work patiently and lovingly toward that end, your children and their spouses may come to view you less as a relic of their past, and more as a gift of fine wine whose value has appreciated with age.

As you show respect for your children and their mates, as you pay attention to who they are and what they want, you must not forget yourself. Give yourself a present, too. Figure out how you can meet your own needs as you allow others to meet theirs. We've been talking about various ways to do this throughout this book, and it's clear that it's not easy. If you are successful, you can expect not only to win your children's respect but many more rewards: growth, appreciation, closeness, caring, intimacy, and love.

A Footnote: The Other Mother as a Gift

The influence a mother-in-law may have in the life of her family, or how much she may be missed if she's not around, is not always evident. Janet's story puts that into clear perspective for us.

Janet was thirty-six when she told me about the gift she missed most: "I have a great sense of sadness that I never met the person who created the man I love. It is a huge loss. I missed not being received into another family, and it has made me feel empty, because my own mother died one year after I married. There is no sense of being able to celebrate. There is a tremendous gap. There is nobody to make a fuss over my children. It's a gift to share the joys of children, and I have neither a mother nor a mother-in-law to share with.

"What comes to my mind, when I hear people complain about their mothers-in-law, is that you need to accept with love all the positive things mothers-in-law have to offer, and be especially grateful for their role as grandmothers, for it's very special. My children never had an intimate connection with another generation — no real strong bond, no chance for the third generation to bridge time and be a child with the first generation. That's a gift I really miss, one that leaves an empty place in my heart."

Your daughter-in-law's birthday is two weeks away. You want to get her a thoughtful gift, but are not sure what she'd like. Since she and your son have been married only a few months, you don't know her tastes very well yet. You decide to:

a. Buy her that nice sweater and skirt you saw on sale at Bloomie's.

b. Give her a $75 gift certificate.

c. Ask her what she'd like for her birthday.

d. Ask your son what she'd like.

e. Buy her the toaster oven you know they need.

f. Buy her the latest self-help best-seller on marriage.

Let's take a look at how each response might contribute to the relationship with your daughter-in-law.

a. You probably don't know her well enough to choose this.

b. This is impersonal but probably would be appreciated by a newly-wed, if the store is selected carefully. Be sure it's seen as a personal gift and not a "grant-in-aid."

c. What a concept! Talk to her!

d. Not a bad idea, but you may not want to make it a habit if you want to build a relationship with her.

e. For her birthday?

f. You don't want to butt in on the relationship this way. Such an item suggests they may need help already. If they do, it probably shouldn't come from — or through — you.

Chapter 9

IMPROVING YOUR IN-LAW IMAGE
It's Time to Become the Person You've Always Wanted to Be

*H*as it really been more than a decade since I watched my children riding bicycles in the streets? My kids are grown and independent now, of course, so they're no longer in my life everyday. That is perhaps as it should be — at least that is as it *is*.

You Gave Them Wings, and They Flew
Growing older, I watched my children become resourceful adults, and that's what I hoped for. But every now and then loneliness descends. You can tell yourself that life isn't over when your children marry, but some days it sure feels like it.

If you complain, "I've lost my children to their lives," it's hard to change. True, you feel tremendous sadness. It doesn't matter that the societal script reads, "Aren't I lucky. My child married such a nice person," if you don't *feel* lucky. You do suffer a loss when you become a mother-in-law, and you have to acknowledge it and go through a process of mourning.

Although it is painful, you have to give yourself permission to separate from your adult children, because separate they must.

What Are You Doing the Rest of Your Life?

But what do I do now that they're gone? I'm part of a generation of mothers that was taught to put ourselves second, to think first of providing a wholesome environment for our children. We bought it. Some of us pretended that what we wanted didn't matter. Some of us even denied we *had* needs. "Oh, I don't need anything for myself." Yes, you did.

Some of us who felt trapped being at home finally broke free when our children were in their teenage years. We attended classes, finished college, obtained a degree, worked. Did all of these accomplishments help? I don't know. I do know it was tough going in those days before dual-career households became a necessity just to make ends meet.

Maybe your own story is like that of many women my age — married, divorced or widowed — who worked when their children were young: "When I went back to work, we weren't given much support. Women who wanted to be independent, or wanted their families to have 'the good life,' went to work outside the home. Many times we weren't sure we were doing the right thing. There was a lot of guilt flying around, and the hope was that we wouldn't later regret working. We didn't know if our children would suffer from our having a career. What we did know was that we had to get out of the house, and told ourselves we were better mothers because we were 'fulfilled.' We found out that if we set our minds to it, we could do much more than we thought we could."

But that's not everybody's story. Then as now, many women did not work outside the home. For some — perhaps you? — finding a niche outside the family was not a goal. They maintained more traditional lifestyles, finding their fulfillment in home and family, perhaps taking part in school, church or community activities.

Of course, there were days for all of us — working and non-working mothers — days when we were overwhelmed, when we wanted to be free, free of responsibilities to family, job, whatever.... On those days, the answer was to talk to a friend. She usually said, "C'mon over. Let's talk." Sometimes tears flowed. Fortunately, there was always a Virginia, a Jane or a Barbara who would give of themselves — real friends who brought out the best in us. Bonds were established, and years passed.

We realize that John Donne was right when he said, "No man is an island, entire of itself." No woman, either.

We discovered we couldn't do it all, fill everyone's needs as well as our own.

(I wonder if young women today really can, or are they juggling as fast — and perhaps dropping the ball as often — as did their mothers and mothers-in-law a generation before?)

"Mirror, Mirror, on the Wall..."

For generations, the only value most women had was in the role of caregiver. Any recognition they received came from being needed by their husbands and children. When their children married, these mothers lost their most valued occupation. Some got bogged down in negative self-talk: "Too late for me now. If I had it to do over again, I'd have a career. If only I were younger..."

Okay, maybe it didn't happen. But your life isn't over. You're simply at a different stage, and big shifts have to be made. You aren't going to live forever, but there's plenty of time to loosen up a little and make a commitment to develop *yourself.*

But *how,* if you've defined yourself only as a caregiver, and perhaps a volunteer or part-time worker?

One way to begin is to take a close look at your relationships with others. If you haven't been getting the responses you hoped for from others, are you willing to look more closely at your part?

Are you pushing people away by doing any of the following?

- Talking too much — going on and on
- Always having the last word
- Blaming

- Speaking in an authoritarian tone of voice
- Acting aloof, which sends the message "I'm not interested in you."

Ask yourself, "What habits do I have that people dislike?" I recognize, for example, that most people resent those who bluntly give advice. (I've given you lots of advice in this book. Of course I want you to agree with me that it's "for your own good," but isn't that what every advice-giver says?) There are times when advice is just the thing, but do keep in mind the basic rule: *save your advice until you're asked for it*. It has a chance of being heard — and maybe even accepted — only when the other person is ready for it (not just because you're ready to give it).

My mother had to "get things off her chest" (her euphemism for criticizing). Unsolicited criticism puts the brakes on any developing relationship. *Best friends* don't even like to be with you when you criticize them. Can you imagine what this does to an *in-law* child?

Others we stay away from are the "poor me" whiners, who see the world as a terrible place and talk about the past as if they lived in a time warp. Ask them a question, and they'll provide a monologue instead of a dialogue. If they ask *you* a question, it sounds as if they're looking for advice; but if you offer suggestions, they usually reply, "Yes, but," and provide reasons why they can't follow through. These people don't nurture themselves — generally speaking, new ideas frighten them.

To be a happy mother-in-law, you need to reduce your reliance on others. You need to become loveable and in touch with *your own* emotional needs. You can't wait for someone else to give you the things you want. *You* have to work at change to get your needs met.

This may sound silly, but to be a person you like, you have to like yourself.

The World Needs Critics...
But You Don't Have to Be One of Them

Earlier generations of parents — probably yours — thought the best way of child rearing was to point out shortcomings. All your mistakes and negative qualities were stressed, so you've learned to identify with your parents' criticism of you: "You're disrespectful. You're lazy. You never..." Many of those messages are still in your head. That's a heavy burden to carry around, and those of us who bear it find it tough to give to ourselves in a healthy way. You may be your own worst enemy.

To be likeable — and, most important, a person *you* like — you must become interested in developing yourself. You've got to rid yourself of those old "critical-parent messages" and begin to acknowledge your strengths and positive qualities.

You have to change your inner criticisms to get rid of the blues, from "people don't care about me" to "people *do* care about me," and give them an opportunity to show it. When we hold back, we signal others to stay away. What signals are you sending?

Release Your Tears

At times, all mothers-in-law feel weepy, but we stuff the feelings of loneliness, uselessness, and sorrow way down. These don't disappear because we freeze-dry them, that only happens when we let them thaw out. It's better not to deny a surge of sadness. It's all right to let yourself feel pain, far better to release tears than to hold them back.

Do you get terribly upset when you see another in distress? This prevents people from feeling their feelings. They compound the error by asking themselves, "What's wrong with me? I'm a strong person."

And your friends, in trying to comfort you when you're depressed, want to make you *stop* crying instead of allowing you to confront your issues.

It's more helpful to permit people to acknowledge their pain. Tears don't equal weakness; tears equal strength. To grieve is to wash away pain. It's like changing the oil in a car: You drain out the old because its powers are spent, and replace it with a fresh supply that protects the automobile, allowing it to function better. Tears help drain the negative emotions to make room for positive feelings.

So give vent to sorrow when those feelings take over. Go to a private place. (The shower works well — no one will hear you grieve or see your make-up run.) Then let yourself go.

For better or for worse, grief is not progressive, but a back-and-forth emotion; you'll have good and bad days. But with time, grief always becomes less sharp.

If you get "stuck", feel hopelessly sad — don't want to get out of bed in the morning, are indecisive and teary *all* the time — it may be a signal that something is terribly wrong, and it's best to seek professional counseling.

All your feelings are normal and part of being human. Experiencing grief, and anger, and fear, and frustration helps us to know ourselves, to become more successful people, to become more fully human, and to be better mothers-in-law.

You'll still feel insecure, anxious, hurt, and lonely at times. But your tears will help you get outside yourself, and you'll have more to offer others.

Moving On

There are lots of specific steps you can take if you really want to improve your life. If you don't like the image you see in the mirror, address the problem. You *can* make yourself more presentable, and once you do something about your appearance, you'll feel better. If you feel stagnant, make a decision to develop a talent you have — photography, music, painting, cooking, needlework, writing. Try meditation to relieve anxiety, write that novel, or go back to school. Or try one of these:

- Travel to that place you have always dreamed of seeing.
- Research your family tree and write down your family history for your children and grandchildren.
- Join a quilting group.
- Teach English as a second language.
- Learn something you always wanted to learn — take a course.
- Read to the blind.
- Join a political organization.
- Volunteer at the library.
- Assist at a day-care facility.
- Become a museum or zoo docent.
- Enlist as a hospital volunteer.
- Check out the needs at the local resource center for senior citizens.
- Get active in your church, synagogue or parish.
- Dig your old instrument out of the closet and join a band.
- Find out about local literacy programs and help others learn to read.
- Ask how you might help out at an elementary school.

Focus on what's happening in your neighborhood, town, or city, and become a part of it.

We human beings are social animals. Mixing with others helps us forget our problems. You'll find that the more you do, the more emotional energy you'll have. Try a new activity even if you don't feel like it; once you get started, you'll become caught up in it.

If you try several activities and don't enjoy them at first, you've learned more about yourself, your likes and dislikes, strengths and weaknesses. And there are always new doors opening up.

One important guideline here: If you are doing things you really *dislike,* stop. When you deny what you like and who you are, you lose a part of yourself. And, after all, a mother-in-law is as entitled to say "no" as anyone else!

Remember the Guy Who Got You into All This

Now may be the time to revitalize a marriage gone stale. With
your children gone, you can be more relaxed at home and focus
on what's special about the man you married. Send him a greeting
card that says, "I miss you," or one that makes him laugh. A couple
I know take long hikes in the woods. What about a luncheon date,
breakfast in bed, or sex instead of supper?

Can you let yourself play? Take a tip from the grandkids. Small
children seem to have a marvelous ability to lie around, doing
nothing. Just being with another child is enough. When asked if
they want to go somewhere, they often answer, "I can't. I'm
playing." Have fun with your mate. Like children, take time to
enjoy just being with him.

Mothers-In-Law have Choices

We all need acceptance, so we sometimes tell ourselves, "People
won't like me if I say no." It could be you value yourself *only*
through the eyes of others. If this is the case, you will cater to
others' wishes — to your own disadvantage, and often to theirs
as well.

People-pleasing impedes growth; ultimately you lose the ability
to discover who *you* are. Perhaps it would be wise to ask yourself:
"What are the realistic risks if I *don't* do what others want, but do
what I'd like instead?"

Driving through my neighborhood, my attention is often
drawn to shop windows displaying brightly colored clothing.
Recently, I spotted a dress, the same shade as my grandson's devil
costume. "Come in," it called.

Without stopping to think, and knowing I looked scrungy that
day, I parked and entered that boutique. Two saleswomen spotted
me, but neither approached. Finally, I said, "I'd like to try the dress
in the window."

"It's very expensive," one replied, whipping past.

I felt my stock tumble down the buyer graph line, and I crumbled. Why didn't I repeat what I wanted? Instead, there I was, a grown woman, a grandmother, doing an about-face.

I had come up short — not to the sales clerk, but to myself. If I'd had more confidence, I could have stayed the course. But instead I acted out in the present unresolved issues of the past. Wanting to be nice, I was looking to please the clerk, and forgot about me.

There were lessons to be learned that helped me know the real person, the one inside who doesn't always feel self-assured and valuable. If I'd asked myself, "Why am I here?" and "What do I want?" the moment I felt uncomfortable, I wouldn't have acted stupidly. If you run out on yourself, you damage *you*. But if you clarify your needs and let people know your expectations, you will be less victimized and more successful.

Commit to Self-Improvement

Are you always passive, thinking in terms of "shoulds" or worrying about next month, concerned about all the things that can go wrong in your lifetime?

Instead of going through the tortures of the condemned, why not take time to work on some of your problems? There are no quick cures, but answering the questions below can help you overcome them. List several answers for each.

- How can I do things "well enough," and not insist they be "perfect"?
- How can I concentrate on what I can have and let go of what I can't?
- What's positive about my life?
- What are some of my needs?

Think about getting rid of negative thoughts to become not only a more effective person, but a happier mother-in-law. What actions can you take? What do you stand to lose if you don't?

What will you gain? The more you work on yourself, the faster you build self-confidence.

Feeding the inner person is like brushing your teeth. You can't brush only once in a while if you hope to have good dental hygiene. To feel alive and build self-confidence, the mind needs affirmations on a daily basis. Think of your strengths, and remind yourself of times you did something that turned out really well. The more you think positively, the more you will change your behavior to act positively. Encourage yourself every day. Do it the way you would if you were talking to a child. Say "That's good," and "You're doing fine."

Reading this book will not change you, just as reading a diet book won't help you lose weight. You have to make the effort. And children, old enough to be married, can take care of their own problems and learn from their mistakes. Sure, they are still part of your life, but they no longer dominate it, and at present, you are not central to theirs. Moreover, directing your thoughts elsewhere will reduce the stress on everyone.

Lessons from the Real World

Stephie, who supervises twelve television writers in an office where scripts have to be prepared for broadcast, finds that certain employees do not like each other, and it shows in their work. At times, her staff refuses to cooperate. They tell her, "It's not *my* job," but the work needs to be completed to meet urgent deadlines.

So Stephie finds herself constantly negotiating with quarrelsome employees, using all her powers of persuasion. She says, "You have to get along with people that you don't especially like; this office is like a family. You don't have to accept other people's agendas, but you have to adapt. Adapting means you know what's going on, but you make the best of it. You say to yourself, 'I don't love the situation, but I'll work with it.'"

As Stephie has taught her staff, you can't always love the circumstances you have to deal with, but you *can* learn to change and, by doing so, make life better.

Marianne's a head nurse in a large teaching hospital who faces life-and-death problems daily. Recently, one of the people on her staff was getting married, and the other women on Marianne's staff were planning a bridal shower. Marianne disapproved of the chit-chat, the taking time away from patients. She called the nurses together. "We have a situation that needs to be improved," she told them, and with problem solving, all mutually agreed to a solution.

Where Do You Go from Here?

Stephie and Marianne are no different from us. We, too, must look at our situations, stop wishing problems away, and do something about them.

Now at last you have time for yourself. After twenty years or more of putting yourself on the back burner, you have time for feeling worthwhile, to start satisfying *your* needs. And the time is right. Middle-aged women are beginning to make their mark in our society, whether running for political office or achieving success in business.

We mothers-in-law aren't yet ready to "go gentle into that good night."

*The nest is empty. You're trying to find ways to fill your days
and nights with something more meaningful than your job. As
you wrestle with the feeling that you've lost your son, your
thoughts are:*

   a. "He'll probably never call me again."
   b. "I don't know what I'm going to do with my life."
   *c. "His wife is nice, but she doesn't know how to take care of
      him."*
   d. "Where did I go wrong?"
   e. "Now I'm all alone, and nobody cares."
   *f. "The children have left — my husband and I have little to
      say to each other."*

When will you start taking care of yourself?

   *a. "Never" is a major exaggeration. He probably won't call as
      often as you like, but be real.*
   *b. That may be true for today, but now you have time to figure
      it out!*
   c If you raised him well, he can take care of himself.
   *d. You didn't. He grew up and became independent — exactly
      what is supposed to happen.*
   *e. If you feel alone it's time to strengthen your relationships,
      find some new friends, try new hobbies/interests/ classes/
      activities,/groups...*
   *f. Now is the time to rediscover why you married your husband
      — and develop some common interests.*

Chapter 10

FRIENDSHIP
Thoughts on the Care and
Feeding of Relationships

*F*ate chooses our relatives, but we choose our friends — people to confide in and exchange ideas with, people who make you feel alive when you're down, people who affirm you.

But first, you have to *be* a friend. Whether with a daughter/son-in-law or someone you've just met, you have to *work* at friendship. You must have something to offer as a friend. You can't be demanding or pushy or you'll scare people away. They'll sense your neediness, feel crowded, pull back.

Friendship is a basic need, but as you get older you may not have as many friends. Casual relationships remain, but become less important as you refine your friendships. You're looking for intimacy.

In this short chapter we'll explore the question, "What is a *friend*, anyway?" The word means different things to each of us, but I think we can agree that friends are those we care about in a personal way, those who reduce our aloneness, those who add value and meaning to our lives. Friends are accepting of one another, steadfast in their mutual loyalty, and compassionate to each other's needs.

Friends also encourage us to be all we can be. As the writer Anais Nin once wrote to her mother, "Each friend represents a world in us, a world possibly not born until they arrive, and it is only by this meeting that a new world is born."

There are many levels of friends, and mothers-in-law need them all — each enriches life in a different way.

Casual Friends

These are your "I'm okay, you're okay," chit-chat friends. We all have such small-talk relationships and know what to expect of them. You enjoy these people when you see them. They are the relatives you send a Christmas card to each year, the neighbors who ask about your children and wish you well.

It's possible to have a casual friendship with a son or daughter-in-law, perhaps because distance separates you, or by virtue of the fact that your in-law child is self-contained and withdrawn. You appreciate what you have; it allows you to feel comfortable, and you interact with him or her the same way you would if you met a friend of a friend at a party.

You may never broach controversial subjects, and your questions and answers may be guarded because you lack trust. Such a relationship is as good as it needs to be; you are acknowledged, though it fails to enrich. Other people may think you're lucky to have such a nice in-law: "At least you get along!" "At least he comes for the holidays!"

A wise mother-in-law knows that sometimes we never can become close with our children's spouses, because they run from intimacy or because we have little in common. The lack of depth you feel is offset by an absence of bad feelings, and maybe this signifies the only level the relationship can be sustained at this time. It may not be intense, but at least it's not hostile!

A casual relationship can be a "good enough" relationship. Appreciate it without a sense of failure. If you've made a genuine effort — tried to meet him/her more than half-way — tell yourself,

"I did the best I could." (If you win third prize in a bake-off contest, it doesn't mean you're deficient in any way.) Accept the limitations of the relationship without disappointment, instead of minimizing what you've accomplished. Continue to show your love for your own child, and your affection for the in-law child, and leave it at that.

A casual relationship with a son- or daughter-in-law may not meet all your needs or expectations, but then does *any* relationship? No bad feelings need rise to the surface, and you both can still get much from your connection — more perhaps than you might expect. Intimacy, after all, is only one measure of the value of a parent-child in-law relationship.

Social Friends

You work, go shopping, argue politics, or play bridge with these people — discussing activities, make-up, and the latest fashions. You share many of their thoughts and opinions and, generally speaking, are emotionally connected, comfortable, and have mutual respect and warmth. This differs from the casual relationship because of its greater involvement. Moreover, even if you view the world differently, it doesn't add hurdles to the relationship. On the contrary, it provides texture.

Social friends, recent or old, accept you for who you are. And you can spend time reminiscing together, because they know exactly what you are talking about when you mention a word. If you ask them, "Can you walk my dog when I'm out of town tomorrow? I hope it isn't an inconvenience," they'll answer, "What are friends for? To *be* inconvenienced."

But something is held back with social friends. You wouldn't tell them your deepest secrets.

Most in-law relationships are social friendships. You have fun, laugh openly, don't walk on eggs or watch your words. And you truly look forward to being together with your married children and your in-law family. All talk comes from the heart. Still, although you would like to, you can't seem to move to an intimate footing, perhaps because of generational, ethnic, or cultural differences. Nevertheless, you have much in common. Maybe sometime in the future you'll share more, but for now the relationship remains rich, and increasingly satisfying — a close facsimile to intimacy.

Try seeing a social relationship as a balloon almost filled with air. If two people push on either side of it, some pressure inside thrusts back, keeping them slightly apart. These friendships have a barrier you can't see or define, yet it's always present, like the air in the almost-full balloon.

Intimate Friends

Intimacy, the deepest level of friendship, defines your closest friends, the ones you can count on your fingers, and with whom you feel emotionally connected at all times. Yet you still feel free. Truly accepting and supportive, intimate friends allow you to know who you are. They may or may not have the same interests, but you have a responsibility for them and to them, a reciprocal feeling of safety, loyalty, trust, honesty, and love.

Intimate friends have your best interests at heart and encourage you to stretch yourself. They see your worth, enthusiastically value your self-development, and share your struggles. A special closeness exists between intimate friends — a closeness that siblings may, but don't always, have. It's a certain chemistry that draws like a magnet.

In intimate friendships, giving and receiving become one. You experience the gift of your friend receiving your giving; and when you receive, that's also a giving, because the other person is feeling the same thing.

Some of us find it hard to accept this kind of relationship, and set up walls which tilt the balance, pushing others out of our lives. By the same token, we don't permit ourselves to truly enter their lives, either.

Intimate friendship requires virtually total openness and hours of work over time. Most relationships never reach this level.

A few mother-in-law/daughter-in-law relationships attain such intimacy. For most of us, however, respect and recognition of differences is as far as the relationship can go.

Don't get impatient with yourself or see it as a sign of failure if you don't achieve this level of closeness. Parents rarely enjoy genuine intimacy with their own children, and it's even more unusual with an in-law child. Some daughters-in-law — and some mothers-in-law — have a fear of closeness. If one's first relationship (with mother and father) was problematic, for example, learning to trust can be tough. Stop expecting perfection, and try to look at the larger picture.

What Kind of Friend Are You?

If you don't have a good self-image, you probably think that you can't bring anything of value to a relationship. Maybe you're asking yourself, "Why would anyone want me as a friend?" Funnyman Groucho Marx didn't even phrase it as a question; he said, "I don't want to belong to any club that would accept me as a member!"

If you want to have friends, you must first *be* a friend. In order to have anything of value to give to a relationship, you must consider yourself something of value. I have no doubt that you are, but *you* may doubt it.

I urge you to make the most of yourself. Talk to yourself about goals. You know what you like and what you're comfortable with, so consider putting your own needs on an equal footing with those of the rest of the family. Provide yourself with a strategy for empowerment, so you can take charge of your own life. Build new skills, make new friends (even casual ones), renew old friendships, fix yourself up, develop a hobby, write a journal, paint a picture.

Take care of yourself; if you don't, who will?

Computer Games

Much of this I've had to learn the hard way: by experience. Looking back, if I had the last decade to do over, I'd have begun using a computer when they first came on the market, instead of making all kinds of excuses: "Too expensive!" "I'm too old." But it's never too late to learn. When I began using the computer, I gave myself encouragement every day. Not being a mechanical person, I had misgivings, but I made a conscious effort to tell myself daily, "You can operate a computer. If you practice, you'll master it."

Still, doubt plagued me. Even though I know a myriad of youngsters who play computer games, I had the feeling that, in my hands, the system would destroy everything I ever wrote — maybe itself too.

My contemporaries reassured me. "It's easy," they said. "Once you get the hang of it, you'll wonder how you ever got along without a computer."

My husband's encouragement provided the final incentive to purchase the hardware and the software. My hands sweated while the computer asked questions, retained files, and told me how to number and print pages.

I had made a commitment to *myself*, so I plowed through the instructions. I enrolled in a class to learn basic computer skills. Sometimes, in nervous agitation, I screamed, "You *will* operate this damn machine!" At times I denounced the machine, but I kept at it because I needed the infernal device as a writing tool.

I didn't have a feeling of competence at the computer for a long time — some things don't make sense until you experience them for awhile. Actually, that process rather precisely mirrors learning the role of a mother-in-law. I'm still not perfect at either.

Others have been there before, but it's not something they can explain. You must experience the role yourself, learning and relearning, doing the work. The good thing is I'm not letting myself be trapped in certain life patterns when I have awkward moments.

What motivated me? Tenacity. Determination. A belief in myself. Knowing that at some point I would succeed. Realizing I'd be richer for the experience. If I gave up, I would have a failure self-image, so I withstood the discomfort.

If I Can Do It, So Can You!

I want to encourage you, too, to take a risk. I don't care if you learn to use a computer, but try becoming a better friend — to yourself, your casual friends, your social friends, your intimate friends, your in-laws, your own children.

• *Start by pushing aside your fear,* or walking right through it. As author Susan Jeffers says, "Feel the fear and do it anyway!"

• *Begin to empower yourself.* Develop new skills in communication, self-assertion, empathy, listening.

• *Make a list of your goals and needs.* Identify several possibilities you'd like to explore. Keep an open mind.

• *Make several action plans.* Start small, but give yourself a number of options to choose from.

• *Don't let minor setbacks stop you.* If Plan A doesn't work out, say, "I can live with this," and get busy with Plan B.

• *To reduce stress, try imaging.* In your mind's eye see a mountain you can climb. Take the first step toward the top. See yourself moving upward on the mountain. Keep taking steps. Slowly. Don't get discouraged if you stumble along the way. Every climb has backward slips. Nobody proceeds through life in a straight line. That's not part of the human condition.

• *Reinforce yourself daily.* Say, "I can handle this," and know that eventually you will succeed. Fulfilling your needs will add spice to your life, and the energy needed to develop a stronger self. Without challenge, there's no possibility of being anything different than you are now.

• *Remember you're not alone.* Many of your peers are having the identical trauma, though most mothers-in-law don't discuss their problems when making polite conversation. Sharing with one another or in a support group, can be a salvation to gaining insights. We mothers-in-law need to open up emotionally and exercise our intellect, because it atrophies with disuse. We need new thinking, sources of involvement, and especially friends, with whom we have more in common than with our children. And when we focus on others and give up worrying about things we can't control, we'll have a better chance of moving relationships forward on a path to intimacy. As you become a better friend to yourself, you'll be a better friend to others without even trying!

Solitude then will no longer mean loneliness. Instead, those quiet moments you used to fear will coax forth reflection and introspection, when you can hear what's going on inside yourself, and that inner peace will lead irresistibly to wisdom.

Most of your friends are parents of your daughter's friends. You've known each other from school activities, overnights, sports. Now the kids are grown; Lisa is married and gone. As you reassess your friendships, you realize you may not see these folks much anymore. You're thinking:

    a. "I won't be seeing my friends any more."

    b. "Things are sure going to be quiet around here without Lisa and her friends."

    c. "None of my old friends call me these days."

    d. "The idea of living the rest of my life alone with Henry is frightening."

    e. "Maybe I should give Elizabeth a call..."

What are friends for?

    a. You can see your friends if you take the initiative.

    b. Things will be as quiet as you allow them to be. You do have a life.

    c. Are you calling them?

    d. What's wrong with Henry? Maybe it's time to ignite the old spark.

    e. Yes! And Janet, and Annabelle, and Martha, and... To have friends, be a friend.

Chapter 11

GROWING
It Takes A Lot Of Loving
To Become Real

I remember the many springs of my childhood, when my family travelled to the country before "the season" began in late June. Apple trees blossomed and fragrant air rose from a greening lawn. My grandparents owned a bungalow colony in the Catskill mountains, and my family lived in one of the older dwellings facing the rutted clay road that wound through the surrounding foothills to the village miles away.

Across from our bungalow, on a deserted lawn, stood a three-story building with lots of rooms and kitchens; beyond was a forest where birds nested. This large building had eight steep cement steps leading to a porch that wrapped around one side. On the porch sat twelve rocking chairs, some painted orange and some green. I didn't see them as garishly bright then, but they were. I saw them only as big and fun to sit on, grounded swings that had room for me and my dolly.

I would awaken early in the morning, when the dew glistened sweet on the grass, plop down from my bunk bed, dress, and steal out of the bungalow. I'd scurry to the other side of the road to the main house where, sitting on the porch in a glorious sunbeam, was Grandpa, a slender man dressed in a shirt with a collar, light trousers, and sturdy shoes. His spare frame fitted comfortably on the seat of a rocker, while gaunt fingers clasped a carved walking stick, as much a part of him as hands to arms. Alone in the quiet he sat, thinking private thoughts, his soft hair blown awry, his shaven face silent, soaking in the golden warmth. But his clear eyes were the most important part of him — for they were the kindest eyes I ever knew.

He smiled as I approached, and he watched me pull my orange rocker closer to his chair, until we almost — but not quite — touched. We sat with arms outstretched, rocked, and looked into the sunbeams, pouring down on us like elongated halos.

I was at peace those summers, though the country was at war.

We'd sit for ten minutes or so; then the bakery truck would cling-clang up from the village. Grandpa stood, reached for my hand, took the carved walking stick, and we would stomp down the steps to where the truck had parked.

The back door askew, a man in a white apron pointed to the shelves that lined the truck, explaining what he had that day. I could see crusty loaves of light and dark bread, numerous rolls, and sometimes raisin buns. It was a wonderful sight for a child of seven, and the fresh smells were bewitching. Grandpa made the purchases, and I got a raisin bun, square-shaped, with white icing on top and soft to the touch.

And then the vision fades. But at those difficult moments in life when I require *something* to hold on to, this image of Grandpa surrounds me like comfortable clothing, healing and soothing, providing the comfort I need.

My grandfather died when I was nineteen, and that memory is so painful I cannot recall his death at all.

But his love crept into my heart, and his warmth made a difference in my life. I want to do the same for my grandchildren today. So do you.

From Experience... Acceptance and Wisdom

As we explore new ideas and develop a stronger sense of self in our mature years, old beliefs fade and we become more accepting. While our grown children struggle to achieve recognition and possessions, we're losing our acquisitiveness: who needs another tablecloth or more vases when our closets are already full? Material possessions become less important. The simple joys give us pleasure — time with family, warmth between the generations, tranquility, trust in a grandson's eyes as his hand reaches for yours, fresh flowers, photographs and, most of all, our children's happiness.

We know the richness of love, and what we actually meant when we promised, "in sickness and in health." We know what's coming — because we have experienced fear and death. We realize that each of us has erred and is fallible. As a result, we've become more insightful, tolerant, gentle — shifting our values toward acceptance, toward preserving family life.

The best part of this new-found wisdom, is that we at last understand there are more important things in life than petty irritations. We've become "bigger" people.

When you face conflicts with the next generation, and you will, *you* can reach down into yourself and take the necessary steps to relate in better ways to your children and their spouses. By letting go of your own childishness, you build a more peaceful world. Your focus changes. You become less involved with the superficial and dig deeper for things that leave you with lasting joy.

Although it takes a big person to back off and look for common needs in the face of conflicts, you must take that path. Truly successful mothers-in-law are those who aim for win-win situations. They avoid both the path of conflict ("You're wrong! You should do it my way.") and the pretense that everything is fine ("Do whatever you want. I don't give a damn.")

Problems approached that way don't get worked on. You harbor resentment, and in the end you'll be unhappy because the conflict isn't resolved and the relationship won't move forward.

Evaluate

If you were leaving on a trip, you'd ask, "What do I need to pack?" then set everything out on the bed. You may wind up with a big pile of clothing at first, but you want to travel light, so you'd put half of it back.

We want to travel light emotionally too, so we have to get rid of grudges, anger, and envy, qualities we don't need, and go about restructuring ourselves. We can all be repaired. And the more we get in touch with our own negative feelings, the more we're able to understand another's side.

We learn to *evaluate*.

Both a wise mother-in-law and son/daughter-in-law know you can't just blurt out everything that comes to mind. When you say whatever comes into your head and don't process thoughts, when you allow the momentary anger you feel in the heat of an argument to explode, you tend to be hurtful rather than constructive or effective.

Words spoken in animosity can't be retrieved, no matter how much you apologize. They resonate for a *long* time. But they don't have to be the *only* words in your head. Why should you continue to hear anger? Instead, get in touch with the memory of hostility and inquire, "Of all the things I could be thinking, why this?" You can then put up a sign in your head that says *STOP*. You take your mind elsewhere, because you know it's unproductive to keep mining the original thoughts.

Of course the thoughts will pop into your head anyway, but you can understand their uselessness. Instead, you can work to build positive responses as you would a muscle. Practice saying *STOP* and replacing the hostile thought with a pleasant one. Eventually, anger and negative thoughts diminish, helping you arrive at a more neutral point — a point from which you can start again.

Sometimes every in-law wants to scream back, to retaliate when deeply hurt. What I'm suggesting is to take a moment, reflect, ask yourself, "Why do I respond to this with such anger?

"Often new hurts cause old ones to resurface. The scab may be picked off a childhood wound — one that occurred at a time when you couldn't protect yourself and had few coping skills. Though you have improved those skills, when the right (or wrong) buttons are pushed, you may go on automatic pilot, repeat an old pattern, and respond in inappropriate ways. There's no denying the hurt you presently feel is real, but the *intensity* of it may bear no relationship to the present trigger.

Instead, wisdom calls you to keep silent, throw out the heavy baggage, and console the part inside that was hurt during your youth. You are no longer a vulnerable child. You are a capable adult who knows how to give up trying to run the show. You have supportive friends with whom to discuss problems, relieve anxiety and cut down on self-limiting behavior. Stretch yourself, grow a little. You'll find you may not then need to focus on the transgressions of your in-law children.

Analyze

As you learn to analyze, to dig deep, you'll learn much about yourself. You'll recognize when you are reacting, not only to the here and now, but to the there and then.

Ask yourself:

- What did my in-law child say or do to make me so angry?
- What does this remind me of?
- What can be going on for my in-law child?
- What can I learn from this?

Your answers may surprise you! Now let go of the excess baggage, and provide yourself with a lighter, more optimistic repertoire. Then ask, *What I can do in the present?*

- What can I do differently now?
- How can I make it better?
- How shall I say this?
- What is the best time for us to talk?

When your son and daughter-in-law are angry with you, when you're the target of their bad feelings, it can help to remind yourself that it's their problem, that it won't help for you to concentrate so much on being hurt. If your aim is to have an intact family, see your daughter-or son-in-law as the people they are. Sometimes, they don't know a mature way to resolve differences, so they become frustrated and angry — immature actions perhaps, but very human, and maybe all they know.

Our own children act out with us in the safe, familiar, traditional way, the same as they did so many years ago. They revert to childish patterns, perhaps not saying "I want what I want when I want it," but coming across that way nonetheless.

But *you* are the adult here, and you don't want to win the battle and lose the war; consequently, you must make the adjustments necessary to keep the family together. If you respond from anger, you will only exacerbate the situation, so you have to have enough resources, when your in-law child (or your own) is shouting, to remain calm and say, "You sound really upset. Let's talk about this another time," and give both the child and yourself time to cool down — days, a week, months, whatever it takes.

In the meantime, carefully examine the state of affairs, *including your role in it,* then make a plan. Ask yourself, "What do I want?" and "What am I willing to do?" and "How will this conflict affect our relationship?" Keep in sight your long-term goal: family togetherness. Then you'll be able to adapt. Slowly. Perhaps painfully. But that's how we survive the potholes of life and come through unimpaired.

If you want to be a good mother-in-law, you can — you're already outgrowing the "failure tapes" in your brain.

While your children are struggling with independence and forming their own nuclear family, you can strengthen ties with your daughter- or son-in-law, not frighten them away. You're learning how to recognize and avoid the old messages in your head, and how you can permit your children and their spouses to be the people *they* want to be.

Making kids into your ideal image — if that were possible — only validates yourself. It does little to nurture their self-reliance. Ultimately, your children's lives have to please *them*, so they don't look back with regret and say, "I should've and could've" or "If it weren't for my parents...."

Anger... and Forgiveness

We must act from strength and forgive our children, because anger festers, filling us with a bitterness that corrodes our insides like poison, and will leave us forlorn and desolate.

And do we want to make ourselves physically ill or harden our hearts and push people away? *Then* what have we won? In the grand spectrum of things, will the issues we are battling over matter?

Here's how to get past malice. First of all *don't personalize criticism*. Take it for what it is, an opinion, not a fact — and our children's opinions can vary from our own. You don't have to accept their judgments as truths. When your in-law child misbehaves or insults you, look at the *information* given. Be fair in evaluating it. Ask, "Is there some truth in this? Does it apply to me? Am I responsible for the way this person sees me?"

For instance, if you invite your daughter and her spouse for a holiday six weeks ahead of the date, and hear hostility in your son-in-law's voice when he responds, "You're always into long-term planning. I can't make a commitment that far ahead. Make your plans without us," you may have to comprehend that he may merely be feeling anxious or trapped, and it comes out as resentment.

Still, you feel terrible — rejected, hurt, perhaps used, because you've given your child so much, and you're asking for little, but if you recall that the couple usually plans at the *last minute*, you can acknowledge you're really wrestling with a conflict of style. The remedy? Identify where the trouble springs from, then back off from an emotionally unpleasant experience. Accept your internal frustration, know it goes up and down like the stock market, repair the damage. . . and *forgive* the outburst. In the best of circumstances, forgiveness isn't easy, and in the worst, it seems an impossible task to undertake, but if you're committed to growth, it's worth doing.

In forgiving, you hand yourself a gift even more than you hand it to another. Forgiving is a journey into the realms of one's own potential, a softening process that allows you to look at who you are, examine the clutter within, and acknowledge your shortcomings. Only then can you forgive others, focus on their positive aspects, take the good with the bad, and accept the fact you can't control circumstances. Your children run their own lives, and if you end your connection with them, you lose much more than you gain. So forgiveness is being smart — it's weighing all the consequences and seeing that your gains exceed your losses.

By opening yourself up and forgiving, indeed, you take a risk. But you also take charge of your life, and even experience yourself more fully by allowing yourself some emotional bruises. You become authentic. The "real person" emerges. If you never chance getting your toes stepped on, you miss the fun of moving in and out on a dance floor.

While the intensity of blow-ups scare people off, if you remain patient, you realize that some old baggage can't easily be washed out of a system, and that people who explode usually act out from a loss of power — real or imagined, from frustration, from fear too, asking for their pain to be respected. Heard. Acknowledged.

Change is threatening to all of us, and hostile people don't usually admit to attitudes that cause problems. But when *you're* feeling stuck, will you scream, use language, or denigrate others? No. You know that louder doesn't mean righter. You do the practical thing — *evaluate and analyze* before you communicate with your adult children. Keep asking, "What's best to do in this situation?" and toss around a few ideas.

Forgiveness goes hand in hand with understanding, and if you determine that others are fragile or stalled in their growth, how can you be offended? Obviously, if you recognize that another human being has limited potential, you don't become impatient, you change your expectations. You adjust your actions to improve the relationship within the scope of the other's limits and start fresh.

Am I suggesting you allow yourself to be walked on? No, that's not what forgiveness means. The road of forgiveness is paved with compassion, patience, acceptance, life experience and serenity. Forgiveness is the ultimate expression of loving and caring and as it grows, you become your "best self."

You need to set boundaries — limits on the relationship. Learn to assert yourself. Get to know the outlines of your own comfort. Figure out what is acceptable; what you will and will not do. You have to be comfortable within your own skin, so you'll want to learn to communicate with yourself before attempting to communicate with the other person. Problems arise when you're not sure of your needs. If you haven't set boundaries, you're likely to become angry at others for pushing you into decisions you don't enjoy.

When you are truly grown-up, you don't let people invade you. You take responsibility for yourself, knowing you cannot change others.

The best thing to do when things get tough is wait until your emotional temperature has cooled. When you're sufficiently calm, matters become clearer. If you can allow yourself to see the whole person, and integrate the good with the bad qualities, time will allow you to focus on the positives.

Don't be quick to write your in-law children out of your life in anger. Instead you make adjustments, see the good they contribute — mend fences, and find a place for them in your family.

The other mother often must put aside unimportant conflicts and think of her children and grandchildren. (You won't be surprised to hear that it is my unshakeable conviction that grandchildren need an opportunity to know their grandparents. My grandfather — whom you met at the opening of this chapter — made the difference in my life.)

Wise mothers-in-law learn to transcend pain and become ambassadors of good will. We acknowledge the fact that life could be a lot worse, and consider the credit side — remembering those good feelings we want to leave our children and — if there are any — our grandchildren.

There Is Life without Grandchildren

If your children can't see themselves raising a family, then you'll have to deal with the painful issue of not being a grandparent and rely on your best character traits to accept their decision. Our kids don't make such decisions based on our needs, but not having grandchildren is a powerful issue that can cause bad feelings between in-laws.

Here is a comment from a mother-in-law I've talked with about this issue:

Lilly said, "I felt sad that I wouldn't ever experience being a grandparent. For me, it was 'how the cookie crumbled.' When you don't have something you learn not to miss it, you fill your life in other ways.

"My children have a right to make their own decisions. They don't have to satisfy me. Their job is to live a productive life without harm to themselves or society, and my job is to adapt to the circumstance life offers."

Lilly has learned to deal with her feelings of disappointment. And you have to do so with someone other than your children, so that your anger doesn't get replayed over and over, as it will if it doesn't get worked through. In some fashion you'll acknowledge the loss to others — a spouse, close friends, the wall — so that the issue isn't always in the foreground. You know, too, that it may surface at times but that you'll get through it. If you choose not to adjust, it will intrude on the relationship with your children.

Not having grandchildren doesn't mean you are not going to have a rich, full life. You'll fill your life in other ways, and avoid blame. Blame keeps the fires of anger alive. If you have a strong desire to be with youngsters, take steps in that direction; goodness knows there are more than enough children to accept all the love you can give. If you want a warm relationship with your children, you accept that having children doesn't fit their lifestyle, and that they have to do what they have to do. This is truly not your business, and to "butt in" is tap dancing on a hand grenade.

You'll need to learn to cope, since the loss gets triggered every time friends whip out snapshots and talk about *their* grandchildren. You can tell yourself it's okay to feel the pain, and know the desire will fade with time.

You can't make your adult children's lives conform to your vision of wonderful. You have to accept *their* definition, even if not having children is part of it.

...And with Grandchildren

My friend Diane, who lives in Boston, is a soft-spoken woman whose eyes glisten when she talks about her Jewish grandmother.

"My *bubbe* (grandmother) died when I was ten," she tells me over tea on a gray afternoon. "She was sixty-two then, young in years, but she thought and looked like an old woman. She had wispy hair with a bun in the back, and she wore a house dress covered with a white apron. She didn't speak English, but she was always there for me. I was special to her. She instilled a feeling of worth in me.

"I want my grandchildren to have that feeling too, to build their self-esteem, especially my granddaughter Erica, who has Rett Syndrome. It's a rare disease that leaves one with uncontrollable hand movements and no speech, but Erica can point to words."

Diane hopes the little girl will really be able to communicate one day. "Now I watch her body language for signs of pleasure and pain, and her eyes that talk. Laugh. Blink. Snap. The only sounds she makes are giggles, and I treasure every one. She *knows* me. When I see Erica after her therapy, I can't tell you what her smile does. My heart hurts. I love all my grandchildren dearly, but she is my first grandchild, and I don't know how long I'll have her."

Diane pauses, and considers the steam rising from her cup. "You know," she says, "grandchildren give us a whole other dimension of love. I can't wait to visit them, and every step forward they make I celebrate. I remember that this is a special accomplishment and I'm thankful for every candle that goes on Erica's cake. And in order to have these special moments with my grandchildren, I've tried to create an atmosphere of respect, of love and trust with my children. I think we all care about each other, but like any other relationship, periodically, ours has to be reevaluated — people change, times change, circumstances change, and mothers-in-law have to conform to what's happening at that moment."

"What I've reacted to in the past and thought important I no longer feel is significant. I look at the big picture and this has made me a stronger human being. I realize I'm capable of giving more."

Diane is passing on the legacy she received from her grandmother to her grandchildren. Isn't this feeling of love what most of us want to leave behind?

When I think of my grandson, that little elf of four, watch his hand grip my fingers, then conjure up the impish smile of his younger sister, who calls me "Yam-ma," my youth returns, stress leaves my face, and I feel cherished. Receiving and giving love come to life without complications, and the world once more cloaks itself in innocence.

Grandchildren welcome us into their lives and make us more human. They reflect who we once were and constitute our last chance to nurture. Our grandchildren are positive and optimistic, make sense of what's senseless, and look to us for acceptance: "Come play with me. Look what I made today."

As you provide a sense of family and offer your grandchildren unconditional love, they'll pour laughter into your heart, and provide you not only with continuity, but with a sense of well-being.

Young and frightened, I sometimes wore myself out being a good mother, wanting to be even better than my own, determined to do everything properly, terrified of my newborn's crying. What had I done wrong, I asked myself if wails filled the tiny apartment. I created a crisis scenario, agonizing over anything out of the ordinary. Was it chicken pox, or the beginning of a rash drawn out of the diaper area into new territory? It wasn't either. "A mosquito bite," the doctor said, when he arrived. "Next time check your screens."

Now I laugh as I recall those years. I recollect my grandmother, who zipped into that same apartment to baby-sit for me, from time to time, peaches-and-cream skin glowing with pleasure at an unexpected coo from her grandson. Little girl ribbons bouncing in her white-gold hair, she'd tell me of how people lived, and how they died of "the consumption" at the turn of the century, of automobiles in the '20s and how Grandpa's Studebaker took the hills.

Other images of my grandparents unravel. Older ones. Blueberries in tin buckets picked on a hot summer's day. Me, scrambling through bushes, eating them dusty from the field, while sweat dripped off Grandma's face. Afterward, jam bubbled on the stove, as Mason jars lined up, purply-blue, one after the other like tin soldiers, to be squirreled away for winter.

How did it all happen so fast? Not so long ago, my children were just children, and now I'm a mother-in-law and have grandchildren of my own. They are my dividends, held "in the round-tower of my heart," as Longfellow's said in "The Children's Hour":

> And there will I keep you forever,
> Yes, forever and a day,
> Till the walls shall crumble to ruin,
> And moulder in dust away!

Our grandchildren let us know there is a place for humanity in this world. They are our historians, and we want to share our stories and our adult children's upbringing, as well as our time left, with them.

But we mothers-in-law must always remember that our grandchildren are not our children. As we have experienced our children, our grown children must experience theirs. At the same time, our grandchildren *can* bring us all together, because what everyone in a family wants is to enrich their lives.

Been There... Done That

You've lived through your own years of career moves and child rearing and nurturing a family. Now, as a mother-in-law, you have to move forward.

You're no longer the most important person in your child's life, and you have to acknowledge that the new spouse is, and accept a lesser role. Moreover, you stop imagining that you can make their decisions, or expect to be included in all their activities, and face reality.

Time is moving ahead; for all that we lament it, we can't deny it, but because we have been exposed to losses and death, we can incorporate slights and sadness into our life. Time, which scares us, also heals us and makes us worldly, so that we can come to terms with our own limitations and with our grown children's foibles.

When we begin to throw away excess baggage, grow enough to truly understand human psychology and who we are, we can let go of pride's corrosive effects, and become more encouraging, kinder to others and ourselves.

Our maturity permits us to enjoy a broader perspective. Because of new ways of thinking and our old common sense, we open our hearts, allow others to get close to us, even if, from time to time, we get hurt. When we truly comprehend that we *all* say things we wish we hadn't, we understand the meaning of wisdom. In "A Psalm of Life," Longfellow wrote:

> *Lives of great men all remind us*
> *We can make our lives sublime.*
> *And, departing, leave behind us*
> *Footprints on the sands of time.*

And isn't that what we wish to do?

Besides, we must admit that at our children's age, we, too — insecure and less thoughtful — lacked understanding. We, too, *with love in our hearts*, made mistakes. Did our parents shut us out? No. They took grief from us, and inevitably, we must now take it from our children.

If we who have lived so many years cannot be accepting of the world's differences, how easily can a young person with limited life experience be accepting of our needs? What do they know of sorrow? About death? We do, and that allows us to be accepting. We realize that most of the work lies on our shoulders, and that if we value our children, we must permit them to see the adults we have become.

And we *are* capable of growing. From time to time, we have to remind ourselves that none of us want to leave this world on a sour note.

We know that emotionally we're further along. Therefore, it's incumbent on us to reduce the hurts that come and go, to see the other's point of view in order to keep harmony within the family.

Choose Connection

Yes, we mothers-in-law have choices to make. To be successful, we have to put aside antiquated needs and grow into a person who is valuable today. We who have become wise elders understand our in-law child's hurts, because we've been there. Although we know we can't always fill their emptiness, we can have patience with them, and hope that they, given time, will also grow.

Because we've matured and accumulated wisdom from life experiences, we are the ones to work for harmony, grapple with ourselves to stay connected, and not give up our children and grandchildren.

Like Odysseus, *we* must be diplomatic. When he journeyed homeward, his resourcefulness enabled him to adapt to many challenges, and not be conquered by any of them. With courage, we, too, can cope with the hazards of life. With love, we can endure the never-ending situations that arise, think through ambivalent feelings, and come up with workable solutions. With growth, we can make the most of our wisdom, accepting, as they are, our children and their mates. We are the ones to fit the family quilt together into a framework so that all the pieces hold fast, even when pressures are pulling in different directions.

We are, after all, the Other Mothers.

Epilogue

*T*his book has offered you many skills to avoid the "seven deadly sins" listed below:

The "Seven Deadly Sins" of Mothers-in-Law

Meddling instead of minding your own business

Overbearing instead of cooperating

Talking instead of listening

Harping instead of understanding

Expecting attention instead of meeting your own needs

Rejecting instead of accepting

Spending money instead of giving of yourself

I hope it has reinforced your resolve to become an "almost-perfect mother-in-law"!

Twelve Traits of Almost-Perfect Mother-in-Law

M is for *maturity* — it's time for you to be the best you can be

O is for *openness* — to new and different people and experiences

T is for *trust* — your children to live their own lives

H is for *honesty* — it's still the best policy

E is for *evenness* — be as fair as you can to everyone

R is for *respect* — for yourself and for others

S is for *sharing* — give your love freely

I is for *independence* — build your own and theirs

N is for *neutrality* — don't take sides

L is for *listening* — do it carefully and non-judgementally

A for *acceptance* — of yourself and your extended family, warts and all

W is for *wisdom* — grow in it

Bibliography

Auden, W. H., *W. H. Auden Collected Poems*. Edited by Edward Mendelson. Franklin Center, Pennsylvania: The Franklin Library, 1976.

Adams, Ramona S., Otto, Herbert A., and Crowley, Audeane S. *Letting Go: Uncomplicating Your Life*. New York: Macmillan Publishing Co., Inc., 1980.

Angier, Natalie. "Study of Sex Orientation Doesn't Neatly Fit Mold." *The New York Times* 18 July 1993.

Avrick, Leah Shifrin. *How In-Laws Relate*. New York: Shapolsky Publishers, 1989.

Bar-Levav, Reuven. *Thinking In The Shadow Of Feelings*. New York:Simon and Schuster, 1988.

Berne, Eric. *Beyond Games and Scripts*. New York: Grove Press, 1976.

Bilofsky, Penny, and Sackarow, Fredda. *In-laws/Outlaws*. New York: Villard Books, 1991.

Blass, Jerome. "In-Law Problems." *The Jewish Standard*, 27 November 1992.

Borysenko, Joan. *Guilt Is The Teacher, Love is The Lesson*. New York: Warner Books, Inc., 1990.

Bowe, Claudia. "You, Him, And *His* Mother." *New Woman*, February 1991.

Bradshaw, John. *Homecoming*. New York: Bantam Books, 1990.

Bradshaw, John. *Creating Love*. New York: Bantam Books, 1992.

Brown, Charles T., and Keller, Paul W. *Monologue To Dialogue*. Englewood Cliffs, New Jersey: Prentice-Hall, Inc., 1979.

Burns, David D. *Intimate Connections*. New York: William Morrow and Co., 1985.

Caplan, Paula J. *Don't Blame Mother: Mending The Mother-Daughter Relationship*. New York: Harper and Row Publishers, 1989.

Casarjian, Robin. *Forgiveness*. New York: Bantam Books, 1992.

Chinen, Allen B. *In The Ever After*. Illinois: Chiron Publications, 1989.

Cocola, Nancy Wasserman, and Matthews, Arlene Modica. *How To Manage Your Mother*. New York: Simon and Schuster, 1992.

Cohen, Betsy. *The Snow White Syndrome*. New York: Macmillan Publishing Company, 1986.

Cudney, Milton R., and Hardy, Robert E. *Self-Defeating Behaviors*. San Francisco: Harper, 1991.

Daniels, Victor, and Horowitz, Laurence J. *Being and Caring*. San Francisco: San Francisco Book Company, 1976.

De Rosis, Helen. *Women And Anxiety*. New York: Delacorte Press, 1979.

Dyer, Wayne W. *You'll See It When You Believe It*. New York: William Morrow and Company Inc., 1989.

Dyer, Wayne W. *Pulling Your Own Strings*. New York: Thomas Y. Crowell Company, 1978.

Elgin, Suzette Haden. *The Gentle Art of Verbal Self-Defense*. Englewood Cliffs, New Jersey: Prentice-Hall, Inc., 1980.

Ellis, Albert, and Harper, Robert A. *A New Guide To Rational Living*. Englewood Cliffs, New Jersey: Prentice-Hall, Inc., 1975.

Fischer, Lucy Rose. *Linked Lives*. New York: Harper and Row Publishers, 1986.

Forward, Susan, with Buck, Craig. *Toxic Parents*. New York: Bantam Books, 1989.

Freudenberger, Herbert J., and North, Gail. *Women's Burnout*. New York: Doubleday and Company, Inc., 1985.

Fromm, Eric. *The Art Of Loving*. New York: Bantam Books, 1963.

Galbraith, Catherine Atwater, and Mehta, Rama. *India Now And Through Time*. New York: Dodd, Mead & Co., 1971.

Gaylin, Willard. *The Rage Within*. New York: Simon and Schuster, 1984.

Genevie, Louis, and Margolies, Eva. *The Motherhood Report*. New York: Macmillian Publishing Co., 1987.

Golomb, Elan. *Trapped In The Mirror*. New York: William Morrow and Company Inc., 1992.

Greenwald, Jerry. *Be The Person You Were Meant To Be*. New York: Simon and Schuster, 1973.

Halberstam, Joshua. *Everyday Ethics*. New York: Viking Penguin, 1993.

Halpern, Howard M. *Cutting Loose*. New York: Simon and Schuster, 1976.

Hubbard, Ruth., and Wald, Elijah. "Dialogue: The Search For Sexual Identity; False Genetic Markers." *The New York Times*, 2 August 1993.

Israeloff, Roberta. "The Sweet Ogre: learning to live with your mother-in-law." *Cosmopolitan*. March 1992.

James, Muriel, and Jongeward, Dorothy. *Born To Win*. Massachusetts: Addison-Wesley Publishing Company Inc, 1971.

Jung, Carl G. *Man And His Symbols*. New York: Doubleday & Co, 1964.

Keating, Charles J. *Dealing With Difficult People*. New York: Paulist Press, 1984.

Kennedy, Eugene. *On Becoming A Counselor*. New York: The Seabury Press, Inc., 1977.

Kennedy, Eugene. *On Being A Friend*. New York: The Continuum Publishing Co, 1982.

Klagsbrun, Francine. *Mixed Feelings*. New York: Bantam Books, 1992.

Kohut, Heinz. *The Analysis Of The Self*. New York: International University Press, Inc. 1971.

Kornhaber, Arthur, and Woodward, Kenneth L. *Grandparents Grandchildren*. New York: Anchor Press/Doubleday, 1981.

Kutner, Lawrence. "Parent & Child: The secrets behind those mother-in-law jokes." *New York Times*. 18 February 1993.

Lerner, Harriet Goldhor. *The Dance Of Anger*. New York: Harper and Row Publishers, 1985.

Lerner, Harriet Goldhor. *The Dance Of Intimacy*. New York: Harper and Row Publishers, 1989.

Liebman, Joshua Loth. *Hope For Man*. New York: Simon and Schuster, 1966.

Longfellow, Henry Wadsworth. *Evangeline And Selected Tales And Poems*. Selected and with an Introduction by Horace Gregory. New York: Introduction Copyright NAL Penguin Inc., 1964.

Mallinger, Allen E., and DeWyze, Jeannette. *Too Perfect*. New York: Clarkson Potter Publishers. 1992.

Malone, Thomas Patrick, and Malone, Patrick Thomas. *The Art Of Intimacy*. New York: Prentice Hall Press, 1987.

Miller, Alice. *Prisoners Of Childhood*. New York: Basic Books, Inc., 1981.

Miller, William A. *The Joy Of Feeling Good*. Minneapolis: Augsburg Publishing House, 1986.

Missildene, Hugh W. *Your Inner Child Of The Past*. New York: Simon and Schuster, 1963.

Oldham, John M., and Morris, Lois B. *Personality Self-Portrait*. New York: Bantam Books, 1990

Oliver, Lucy. *The Meditator's Guidebook*. Vermont: Destiny Books, 1991.

Paul, Lois. "The Mastery Of Work And The Mystery Of Sex In A Guatemalan Village" in *Woman, Culture, And Society*. Edited by Michelle Zimbalist Rosaldo and Louise Lamphere. Stanford: Stanford University Press, 1974.

Pearsall, Paul. *The Power Of The Family*. New York: Doubleday, 1990.

Peck, M. Scott. *Further Along The Road Less Traveled*. New York: Simon and Schuster, 1993.

Peck, M. Scott. *A World Waiting To Be Born*. New York: Bantam Books, 1993.

Reich, Wilhelm. *Character Analysis*. New York: Farrar, Straus and Giroux, 1945.

Rogers, Carl R., *On Becoming A Person*. Boston: Houghton Mifflin Company, 1961.

Rubin, Lillian B. *Just Friends*. New York: Harper and Row, 1985.

Rubin, Theodore Isaac. *Reconciliations*. New York: Viking Press, 1980.

Sachs, Brad E. *Things Just Haven't Been The Same*. New York: William Morris and Company Inc., 1992.

Sills, Judith. *Excess Baggage*. New York: Viking Press, 1993.

Simon, Sidney B., and Simon Suzanne. *Forgiveness*. New York: Warner Books, 1990.

Tanner, Ira J. *Loneliness: The Fear Of Love*. New York: Harper and Row Publishers, 1973.

Urlin, Ethel L. *A Short History Of Marriage*. Detroit: Singing Tree Press, 1969.

Viorst, Judith. *Necessary Losses*. New York: Fawcett Gold Medal, 1986.

Williams, Margery. *The Velveteen Rabbit*. New York: Simon and Schuster, 1983.

Williamson, Marianne. *A Return To Love*. New York: Harper Collins Publishers, Inc., 1992.

Witkin, Georgia. *Passions*. New York: Villard Books, 1992.

Woodman, Marion. *Addiction To Perfection*. Toronto: Inner City Books, 1982.

Yanagisako, Sylvia Junko. *Transforming The Past*. Stanford: Stanford Press, 1985.

Young-Eisendrath, Polly. *You're Not What I Expected*. New York: William Morrow and Co., 1993.

Other Sources

The Cambridge Encyclopedia Of India, Pakistan, Bangladesh, Sri Lanka, Nepal, Bhutan And The Madelenes. 1st ed., s.v. "How people live."

Encyclopedia Americana. International ed., s.v. "Marriage."

Index

Advice-giving, 6, 8, 34-36, 123, 178
Anger, 131, 203-206
"A Psalm Of Life," 211

Chanukah, 52-54
Chinese American Intermarriage, 51
Chinese culture, 60-64
Christmas, 52-54
Commitment, 91-92
Communication, 5-12, 50-51, 115-116,
    138-139
    being specific and, 126-127
    the blame game and, 119-121
    "December Dilemma" and, 52-54
    feeling talk and, 128-130
    "I Messages" and, 131-138
    listening and, 39, 121-124, 130
    magical thinking and, 116-119
    non-verbal, 125-126
    straight talk and, 124-125
Conflict resolution, 5-11, 199-203
Criticism, 179
Cuban culture, 81-84
Customs, cultural, 51-54, 84-86
    marriages and, 57-60, 86-87
    See also Individual cultural listings

Daughter-in-law, 20-24
    holidays and, 24-25
    interviews, 37-48
"December Dilemma," 52-54
Defense mechanisms, 166-169
Dinkmeyer, Don, 99
Divorce, 92, 96-100
Donne, John, 177

Elgin, Suzette Haden, 119
Ethnicity And Family Therapy, 61, 74,
    76
Expectations, 33-36, 141-146
    unexamined, 149-154
    unrealistic, 147-149

Fairy tales, 3-4
Family quilt, 15-16
Family rituals, 51-54
Family scripts, 17, 20-27
Feelings, 128-139, 179-180
Friendship, 187-191, 193-194
Fromm, Erich, 86

Gay/lesbian lifestyle, 100-113
Gifts, 157-162
    accepting, 163-164
    checklist for, 170
    defense mechanisms and, 166-169
    relationship building and, 171-172
    returning, 162-163
    traditions and, 165-166
    women and, 164-165
Grandchildren, 93-94, 206-210
Greek culture, 73-75
Grief, 179-180
Growth, 175-177, 197-198, 210-212
    acceptance and, 199
    anger/forgiveness and, 203-206
    conflicts and, 5-11, 199-203
    grandchildren and, 206-210
Guatemalan culture, 77-80

Herz, Fredda M., 76
Holiday celebrations, 24-25, 52-54, 137
Homosexuality. See Gay/lesbian
    lifestyle
How You Feel Is Up To You!, 99

"I Messages," 131-138
Indian culture, 69-72
Integrity, 9-12
Interviews, daughter-in-law, 37-48

Ja, Davis Y., 61
James, William, 134
Japanese culture, 64-68
Jeffers, Susan, 193

Kitzinger, Sheila, 79
Kostopolous, Nick, 73

Listening, 39, 121-124, 130
Living together, 93-96
Longfellow, 210, 211
Loss, 2, 175
Lubavitcher Hasidim culture, 75-77

McKay, Gary, 99
Magical thinking, 116-119
Marriage, 3-4, 20-24, 57-60, 86-87, 182
Marx, Groucho, 191

Naruhito, Crown Prince, 65
Necessary Losses, 10
Nin, Anais, 188
Non-verbal communication, 125-126

Odysseus, 212
Ono, Yumiko, 66
Owada, Masako, 65

Parents And Friends Of Lesbians And
   Gays (PFLAG), 112
Patterns, past, 3, 17
Paul, Lois, 78, 79
Plato, 146
Pope, Alexander, 36

Rhasha, Vendaya, 69
Rockwell, Norman, 36
Rosen, Elliot J., 76

Self-assessment, 176-178
Self-awareness, 144-146
Self-improvement, 180-184, 193
   See also Growth
Shon, P., 61
"shoulds/oughts," 19, 141-142, 146-147
Sung, Betty Lee, 51

Tan, Amy, 62
The Art Of Loving, 86
"The Children's Hour," 210
The Gentle Art Of Verbal Self Defense,
   119
*The Greeks: The Dilemma of Past and
   Present,* 73
The Joy Luck Club, 62
"The Mastery Of Work And The
   Mystery Of Sex In A
   Guatemalan Village," 78
The Rituals Of Dinner, 71
The Velveteen Rabbit, 1, 11
Toonkel, Felice, 11, 19
Tu-hsiu, Ch'en, 139

Unmet needs, 16-17

Viorst, Judith, 10
Visser, Margaret, 71
Visual imaging, 29

Wall Street Journal, 66
Weddings, 18-19
Welts, Eva Primpas, 74
Williams, Margery, 1
Woman, Culture, and Society, 78
Women as Mothers, 79

Zotos, Stephanos, 73